FERRETS!

A Fun & Care Book

FERRETS!

**For Today's Pet Owner
From the Publishers of**  **Magazine**

Karen Dale Dustman

photographs by Reneé Stockdale

BOWTIE™ PRESS

Irvine, California

The black-footed ferret photo on pages 6 and 13 is courtesy of Wyoming Game and Fish Photo.

The ferrets in this book are referred to as *he* or *she* in alternating chapters unless their gender is apparent from the activity discussed.

Nick Clemente, special consultant
Ruth Berman, editor-in-chief

Library of Congress Cataloging-in-Publication Data

Dustman, Karen Dale.
    Ferrets! : for today's pet owner from the publishers of Ferrets
USA magazine / Karen Dale Dustman ; photographs by Reneé Stockdale.
        p.   cm. -- (A Fun & care book)
    Includes index.
    ISBN 1-889540-00-5
    1. Ferrets as pets.   I. Title.   II. Series.
SF459.F47D87   1998
636.976'628--dc21   97-32168
                                                                          CIP

BowTie™ Press
3 Burroughs
Irvine, California 92618

Manufactured in the United States of America

First Printing April 1998

10 9 8 7 6 5 4 3 2 1

Acknowledgments

In writing this book, I have discovered just how warm and giving ferret folks truly are. This is my heartfelt thank you to Dr. Deborah Briggs, Jeanne Carley, Dr. Diane Cosko, Chrissy DeNayer, Dr. Deborah Kemmerer, J. C. Matalon, and Diane Rogers for reading drafts, sharing background material, making terrific suggestions, and answering innumerable questions. I could not have completed this project without their kind assistance.

Special thanks are due to Dr. Tom Greek and to Micki Wingate, who endured repeated rough drafts and phone calls with grace and humor.

While each and every one of these wonderful people did their very best to point out mistakes and suggest corrections, the responsibility for any errors that may remain is, of course, purely my own.

Although legal issues are touched on in several places in this book, please be aware that it is not intended to be relied on as legal advice. The legal status of ferrets in some parts of the country is in flux and may well continue to be so. Questions about your particular situation can best be answered by a lawyer in your state.

I wish I could introduce you personally to Reneé Stockdale, the artist behind the beautiful photographs in this book. Although I didn't know her before I began this project, Reneé became a special friend by the time we finished. I am so fortunate to have had her feedback, suggestions, and constant enthusiasm! Special thanks, also, to Pets International, Ltd., and Marshall Pet Products for generously providing products for these photos.

Above all, I'd like to wish a "weasel war dance" of happiness to you, the reader of this book. May your ferrets always be dancing.

—K.D.D.

I would like to thank Micki Wingate of Checker Farm Ferrets; Kristin and Micki from Pet Stop of South Lyon, Michigan; The Humane Society of Huron Valley; Shannon Valley Ferrets; and the human models Amy McDonald, Dr. Mark McDonald, Marti Jo Blackwood, Myia Blackwood, Keli Quigley, Robin Meinicki, Jake Meinicki, Trevor Meinicki, Jerid McDonald, Maxine Harris, and Ken Harris for their assistance with this book. Special thanks to the ferret models Gabriel, Possum, and Perry.

—R.S.

Contents

A Nod to Ferret History

1

Friendly, frisky, and inquisitive, domestic ferrets are relative newcomers to the American pet scene. But they're hardly new human companions. According to some sources, the domestic ferret's long and illustrious history may date back as far as 3000 B.C., when the ancient Egyptians used them to hunt rodents in granaries.

Although subsequent details of the domestic ferret's history remain sketchy, they reportedly were popular in ancient Greece and Rome and won fame (if not fortune) helping Augustus Caesar combat an overabundance of rabbits in the Balearic Islands. Some historians speculate that returning Crusaders brought the domestic ferret home to Europe; others say it was the Romans or the Normans. In the thirteenth century, Genghis Khan was a ferret fancier, and in the fourteenth century, King Richard II of England granted his subjects licenses to use ferrets to hunt rabbits—provided they didn't hunt on Sundays.

In more recent times, Queen Victoria kept a group of pampered albino ferrets in royal style, presenting them as gifts to special friends. Sometime around 1875—or perhaps even earlier—ferret pioneers came to the New World, likely serving as rat catchers aboard sailing ships.

Ferrets' earliest association with people probably was in a working capacity. Their lithe, sinuous bodies are perfect for "ferreting out"

Queen Victoria treasured her albino ferrets, like the ferret pictured here, and ordered extravagant cages to be built for them.

mice, rats, and other agricultural or domestic pests, and people quickly figured out ways to use ferrets to help hunt rabbits and other game.

Throughout history, people have taken advantage of the predatory nature of ferrets by using them to hunt game and control the rat population.

Around the turn of the twentieth century, one entire town—New London, Ohio—was nicknamed Ferretville because of the number of ferret breeders who lived there. During the area's heyday, an estimated 40,000 ferrets a year were raised and shipped out by rail to destinations across the country. Shipping companies bought from fifty to one hundred ferrets at a time to keep wharf rats in check. Other customers were farmers and hunters. One Ferretville breeder reportedly cleared $30,000 a year selling ferrets to hunters—a goodly sum in those days.

Not surprising for critters related to the mink and ermine, ferrets' sleek and silky pelts have also been prized by the fur industry. One researcher speculates that Jason's Golden Fleece was actually the pelt of a sable, a close relation of the ferret. As late as 1950, some 400,000 ferret and polecat furs were being sold around the world.

Today, ferrets are weaseling their way into a growing number of American hearts and houses as pets. Intelligent, playful, fastidious, and quiet, ferrets integrate well into homes ranging from city apartments to Hollywood mansions. Like cats, ferrets can be playful and independent. Like dogs, ferrets are affectionate and can be taught to do tricks.

Still, caring for a pet ferret is not the same as caring for a cat or dog. Many of a ferret's needs and behaviors are different from those of other kinds of pets and may take a little getting used to if you have not had the joy of living with a ferret before.

Whether you're considering adopting your first ferret or you just want to fine-tune your ferret parenting skills, this book is designed to help you give your ferret the very best care. Let's start with the basics.

The Natural Ferret

Scientifically known as *Mustela putorious furo*, ferrets are one of seventeen species in the weasel family, a group that includes ermine, mink, and polecats. Other more distant relatives of the ferret include the marten, sable, badger, and otter.

Familiar as ferrets are today as pets, their ancestral origins remain shrouded in mystery. Some authorities believe domestic ferrets are descended from the steppe polecat, while other experts contend they are more likely related to the European polecat, with which they can interbreed. There is also speculation that the Asiatic and European polecat species themselves had a common ancestor before the Ice Age split the population into separate geographic groups.

The playful otter is a distant relative of the ferret.

Because domestic ferrets are, as the name implies, a *domesticated* species, it's impossible to study them in the wild. And it may not be scientifically accurate to correlate

The ferret's relative the wild polecat wears a distinctive mask around the eyes. The two species can be crossbred; in fact, the first domesticated ferrets probably came from the captive breeding of European polecats.

the behavior of one species with that of another, however close they may be on the family tree. That said, an examination of the habits of two of the ferret's close relatives, the European polecat and the ermine, reveals some striking similarities to our captivating companions.

European polecats feed primarily on small mammals such as mice, rats, and voles. They live in other animals' burrows or in tunnels they create themselves. European polecats are nocturnal and have relatively poor eyesight, so they rely heavily on their senses of smell and hearing as guides. Polecat young romp and tussle for a good many of their waking hours and investigate their surroundings by smelling objects they encounter. The polecat's enemies include owls and other large raptors, wolves, and foxes. During an attack, polecats bite tenaciously and release scent from their anal glands. The scent from these glands is also used to mark their territory.

Ermines similarly feed on mice, rats, hamsters, moles, and other small mammals, only rarely eating plants. Ermine nests may be either above or below ground and are lined with a soft layer of grass, twigs, hair, and other materials. Although their eyesight is good in daylight, ermines are primarily nocturnal animals. They are good jumpers, and their bounding run has been compared to a gallop. When traveling at a more relaxed pace, ermines adopt a mincing gait of tiny, fluid steps. The sounds ermines make range from a snarling hiss or scream during an attack to coos or squeals when interacting with other ermines. Young ermines enjoy playing and tumbling with each other and with their mother. Ermines also release scent when frightened or in pain or to mark territory, but they generally do not do so during an attack. Ermines kept as pets will investigate drawers, pant legs, and every nook and cranny in a room.

Ferrets, like other domesticated animals who have been selectively bred for certain characteristics, probably retain vestiges of the behavior of their wild forebears. Their intense, curious investigation of any new surroundings and desire to inspect holes and tunnels are but two examples of possible holdovers from ferret ancestors of long ago.

The Black-Footed Ferret

Although similar in name, the endangered black-footed ferret (*Mustela nigripes*) is actually a different species than its smaller domestic "cousin" *Mustela putorius furo.*

Black-footed ferrets used to thrive across the western Great Plains states and southern Canada. But along with settlers and agriculture came efforts to eradicate prairie dogs, the black-footed ferret's main source of food. Outbreaks of canine distemper compounded the plight of these beleaguered wild ferrets. By the late 1970s, some researchers feared the black-footed ferret was extinct.

In 1981, however, a rancher's dog caught a male black-footed ferret,

and hope surged that a few members of this species still remained in the wild. Exhaustive tracking efforts began, and in 1986, the last seventeen black-footed ferrets found in the wild were captured and brought into a captive breeding program run by the Wyoming Game and Fish Department. Today, there are several hundred black-footed ferrets in captivity. Efforts are under way to reintroduce captive-bred ferrets into the wild. Unfortunately, the breeding program itself is now in danger due to funding cuts.

If you are interested in learning more about the status of the black-footed ferret, the breeding program, and the efforts to reintroduce these animals into the wild, contact the Wyoming Game and Fish Department, 5400 Bishop Boulevard, Cheyenne, WY 82006-0001, or call (307) 777-4600.

Choosing a Ferret Companion

2

Thinking it Through

Choosing a ferret companion can be a fun and exciting process. Perhaps you've fallen in love with a particular ferret at your pet store already. But before you bring a ferret home, there are a few points to consider carefully.

With black legs, tails, and masks, sable ferrets resemble wild polecats in color.

Be sure a ferret really is the kind of animal you want. Owning a ferret is not the same as owning a dog or cat. Ferrets' curiosity, playfulness, and energy can be charming but also make them tough to keep up with at times. Ferret proofing your house is necessary for both the ferret's sake and your own. And while most devoted ferret fans don't find the odor (which can be minimized with bathing and other steps) objectionable, ferrets do have their own very special smell. Make sure you know what to expect.

And before you get too far, make sure ferrets are allowed where you live. It's not legal to keep ferrets as pets in California, Hawaii, the District of Columbia, and some cities and counties. In addition, if you are renting, ask about the landlord's pet policy before you bring a ferret home.

Consider the time and money that caring for a ferret requires. Ferrets are not low-maintenance, low-cost pets. Food and grooming products are not outrageously expensive, but they do add up. Ferrets also require and deserve daily attention from their owners, a responsibility that includes food, water, and litter changes, as well as playtime. They generally live six to eight years, although some hardy old-timers make it to eleven. Are you ready to make such a long-term commitment? Ferrets also require regular care from a veterinarian, particularly as they age. Veterinary bills can be as high as those for a cat or dog. Be sure your budget can accommodate those expenses.

You'll need to budget money for food, grooming, and health products, as well as toys for your ferret.

Don't forget to consider the existing members of your household. Although ferrets often make friends with cats and dogs, an adjustment period (and some effort and patience on your part) may be required. As carnivores (meat eaters), a ferret is not likely to be a safe addition to households that already contain birds, rabbits, rodents, or reptiles. On the flip side, dogs bred or raised as hunters may mistake a ferret for a game animal. It's not a good idea to try to mix inherently hostile species.

A few cases have been reported of a ferret severely biting a very young child when they were left together unsupervised. Although such instances are extremely rare, families with babies may want to delay acquiring a ferret for two or three years. And as with any pet, ferrets should be supervised even with older children when they are playing together.

If allergies are a problem for you or someone in your household, try to find out more about the severity of the person's reaction to ferrets before you bring that adorable fuzz ball home. Some people with allergies find ferrets less of a problem than other pets, perhaps in part because of their smaller size. Ferrets also are reported to have less allergy-triggering dander than cats or dogs. For truly devoted ferret fans, allergic reactions can be minimized by bathing the ferret regularly and by keeping his bedding, cage, and play areas scrupulously clean. Your veterinarian may be able to recommend special anti-allergy grooming products. Air purifiers also may help.

Some prospective ferret owners worry that a single ferret might get lonely without another ferret around for company. Ferrets are gregarious critters and enjoy socializing with humans as well as with each other. If you are away from home during the day or have only limited time to spend with your ferret, you may want to consider adding a second ferret to your family so the two can keep each other company. Some people can't seem to stop at two and find themselves with three or even more!

It's not necessary to acquire all your ferrets at the same

Given some time, ferrets and other house pets usually establish trust and comfort zones.

time, however. Younger ferrets sometimes adapt more readily to having a new ferret in the household than do older ones. But even a ferret getting on in years will usually make the adjustment, given a little time. Your patience and the ferret's natural sociability will usually win out. Some older, stubborn ferrets, however, never do make the adjustment.

Take advantage of the ferret's sociable nature. Two ferrets can be twice the fun!

If you do decide to add a ferret to your family later on, it's a good idea to quarantine the new arrival in separate quarters for two weeks or so to give him some time to adapt to his new household and to make sure he is healthy.

Once the quarantine period is over, you'll want to introduce the ferrets slowly. Move the two cages close together and swap the ferrets' bedding to allow them to get used to each other's scent. Supervise the initial encounters between your ferrets closely, and give them several days to adapt to each other before putting them in the same cage together.

Before getting a ferret (or two) you need to have a plan in case your circumstances change. Life sometimes throws us a curveball. What would happen if your job required you to move to a state where ferrets are not legal? Or what if your own health or living situation made it impossible for you to look after your ferret friend? A humane society may be able to find a new home for your ferret, but all too often unwanted pets wind up being euthanized. If possible, line up a friend or relative who will take care of your pet if the need should ever arise. There are also ferret shelters and rescue groups in every state who may be able to help.

Choosing a Pet Ferret

When it comes to choosing the right ferret, you'll have some fun choices to make. Male or female? What color or pattern? The most important consideration, however, is the ferret's health. Pick an animal with a healthy-looking coat and a good disposition. Signs of a health problem can include discharge from the ferret's eyes, a runny nose, broken whiskers, or feces soiling the fur. Also check the ferret's anal area—a protruding pink membrane could

It's a good idea to include your children when choosing a pet.

indicate a prolapsed rectum, a condition that sometimes requires surgery to correct. The animal should be bright, alert, and gentle, never lethargic or aggressive.

Baby ferrets, called kits, can be a little nippy—it's their way of playing. Just as puppies tug and tussle, baby ferrets stage mock battles and pretend attacks. But playful nipping is different from hard biting. Avoid a ferret who bites hard enough to draw blood.

You'll need to decide whether you prefer a male or a female ferret. Males are larger, growing to be about 4 pounds, while adult females are about half that weight. Males typically have a wider face than females. But there is not a great deal of difference in personality or behavior between the sexes.

Ferrets have a wide range of coloration and markings. The names given to the patterns may vary depending upon where you live. Organizations that sanction ferret shows such as the American Ferret Association (AFA) and the League of Independent Ferret Enthusiasts (LIFE) have established their own standards for each variation they recognize.

Of course, a ferret's color is in his fur. Ferrets have a double coat that consists of soft underfur and longer, coarser guard hairs. Since the underfur is always light, it is the color of the guard hairs that determines a ferret's basic color name. Guard hairs may be black, red, or gray, but are often various shades of brown or white, resulting in color names such as chocolate, sable, cinnamon, and champagne.

This butterscotch ferret's color is determined by the long guard hairs.

This is a sable-colored ferret with a patch pattern, so this ferret is called a sable patch.

The ferret's pattern name is determined by the location and amount of white in his fur. A mitt, for example, has white feet, while a ring-neck has a circle of white fur around his neck. Other distinctions are made based on the density of the ferret's coloration. Pattern names include blaze, panda, and Siamese.

Where to Buy a Ferret

Once you've decided to purchase a ferret companion, you're likely to have several sources to choose among, including pet stores, local breeders, and ferret shelters. Whichever option you choose, look for a clean facility and knowledgeable personnel. Before you make your purchase, check the fine print of any contract you're asked to sign and ask about return policies and health guarantees. Don't shop strictly on price. Like other too-good-to-be-true deals, a bargain ferret may not really be much of a bargain.

This sable ferret is bred not only for color and health, but for temperament as well.

Pet stores that carry ferrets often have kits available year-round. Look for a store that has been in business for many years—an established shop is more likely to stand behind its sale if difficulties arise and can be an important source of information at the time of purchase and in the future. Ask the salesperson about the breeder's experience and reputation. And to really do your homework, also ask for the names and phone numbers of previous ferret purchasers. Taking the time to check references can save much heartache later.

Local ferret breeders are another good source. Small-scale or hobby breeders often take up breeding because they truly love and enjoy ferrets themselves. Their experience with ferrets can make them an excellent source of information. However, these breeders usually have kits for sale only from May through October.

A quality breeder is concerned with not only raising healthy animals, but also breeding for temperament to ensure the kits will be sweet-natured, gentle pets. He or she should be able to tell you a ferret's exact birthday and the personalities and medical histories of the parents. You may want to find out how long the breeder has been in business and ask to see a copy of his or her business and/or USDA license.

Most good breeders are willing to take a ferret back within a reasonable time after the sale if you are unhappy with your new pet, although their idea of a reasonable time and yours may differ—a good subject to discuss before the purchase! Although the transaction may take place in an informal setting, don't forget to insist on a written contract of sale.

Adopting a ferret from a ferret shelter or rescue organization is a third option. Shelter personnel are dedicated individuals who are often quite knowledgeable about ferrets. Although shelter ferrets are apt to be adults rather than kits, they still make great pets and have probably outgrown any boisterous baby tendencies. As an added bonus, they may be litter trained already!

Find out how long the ferret has been at the shelter, and what (if anything) is known about his history and medical needs. Most shelters make certain a ferret's vaccinations are up to date, but it doesn't hurt to ask when the next shot(s) should be given. Be sure you get a written record of any vaccinations the shelter has administered.

Wherever you purchase your ferret, don't be afraid to ask questions. And be sure that the people you speak with will be willing to answer any additional questions that come up later.

Ask a lot of questions when purchasing a ferret. The staff at a ferret shelter is often knowledgeable and should be able to tell you how long a ferret has been there and when he was last vaccinated.

Spay and Neuter Considerations

Ferrets have some unique attributes that make spaying or neutering (altering) an especially wise decision. If an unaltered female ferret (a jill) goes into heat but isn't bred or taken out of heat by a hormone injection from a veterinarian, she will stay in heat. This particularly cruel biological twist can lead female ferrets to develop aplastic anemia and septicemia, serious medical conditions that result in death in up to 90 percent of the cases. Even though an unaltered, unbred male ferret (a hob) won't experience heat as a life-threatening event, his odor and seasonally aggressive behavior toward other ferrets can make him an unappealing housemate.

Unless you plan to devote yourself to breeding ferrets, like this breeder has, altering your pet is essential to his or her health.

Altering your ferret will help prevent the development of the overpopulation problems that are so prevalent with cats and dogs. Even though pet ferrets are far fewer in number than cats and dogs, a quick visit to any ferret shelter will confirm that unwanted ferrets do exist. As an additional benefit, altering helps reduce a ferret's musky body odor.

If you are tempted to keep your ferret intact for breeding purposes, think twice. Breeding is far more complicated than it may sound, and a female ferret's very life is at risk. Some local ordinances require ferrets to be altered unless you hold a special breeder's permit, and zoning and other restrictions may prohibit breeding in some residential areas.

There is some controversy over the proper age at which ferrets should be altered. Some people fear that early spay or neuter surgeries may lead to health problems later on in a ferret's life. Others are just as convinced that there are no adverse side effects and argue that a kit's resiliency promotes quick and successful healing.

Most kits come from the breeder already altered. If you are considering buying an unaltered ferret, ask your veterinarian's opinion about the proper age for the operation, and make sure you know exactly what it will cost.

How Important Is De-Scenting?

Ferrets, like skunks, have a pair of anal scent glands that help repel enemies. Unlike skunks, ferrets cannot spray from their scent glands, but when angry or frightened they do emit several drops of unpleasant-smelling fluid called musk. Although the scent disperses fairly quickly, some people feel ferrets make better company when they have been de-scented. Most ferrets offered for sale in pet stores already have been de-scented.

The de-scenting operation involves removing the ferret's scent glands. A growing number of people feel this surgery is unnecessary unless there is a medical reason to have it done, such as the scent glands becoming plugged. If you find a ferret for sale who has not been de-scented, you may want to talk with your veterinarian about both the advisability of such surgery and its cost. De-scenting certainly is not mandatory, and it *does not* mean that your ferret will no longer have an odor. De-scented ferrets still smell like ferrets.

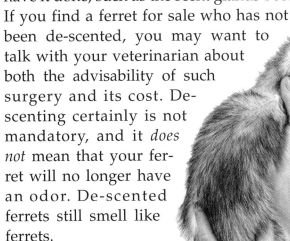

Although a ferret will always smell like a ferret, some people do not mind the musky odor.

Ferrets have a normal musky body odor that comes from sebaceous (oil) glands in their skin. Because sex hormones play a part in this odor, an unaltered ferret will have a much stronger body odor than an altered ferret will. This is especially true with males.

Bathing a ferret and changing his bedding will help minimize a ferret's odor. There are also a number of grooming products on the market, including ferret shampoos and deodorizing sprays, that can help.

Home Sweet Home

3

I t doesn't need to be a castle, but you'll want to make your ferret's home as comfortable as possible. Here are some tips for assembling the basics for a good home, plus a few possible extras.

Cage Comfort

Polecats, one of the ferret's undomesticated relatives, make their homes in underground dens. And although a ferret couldn't survive in the wild, even one who has never set paw out-of-doors still loves to burrow. Your cage setup should provide your ferret with clean, comfortable quarters and allow space for hideaways. A wide variety of cages, bedding, hammocks, and hideaways are commercially available, or if you are handy, you might try making them yourself.

A plastic water bottle is a wise choice for preventing spilled water and wet bedding.

Ideal ferret cages are tall, sturdy, and made of wire. Locks and doors must be secure; ferrets are puzzle-solvers who will try to find an escape.

Metal cages are usually more practical than wooden ones, which absorb stains and odors and can be chewed. Ferrets can slip through surprisingly small spaces, so be sure the grid is small enough (smaller than 1 square inch) that your ferret can't engineer an escape. Check all corners and seams to be sure there are no sharp edges. Resist the temptation to house your ferret in an aquarium, even though the glass sides would seem to display your pet to great advantage. Aquariums do not provide proper ventilation, and heat can build up inside.

Buy the largest cage you can afford. The minimum size for one ferret is 3 square feet. An adequate cage should provide room for the ferret to stand up and move around comfortably and maybe do a little romping and stomping. It's a good idea to consider allowing for a little extra room to expand, too. Kits grow quickly, and who knows, you may want to add a second ferret some day.

For owners, the name of the game with cages is easy cleaning. Look for doors that are large enough for you to reach through comfortably. Also check latches to be sure they are easy to operate and secure. Some ferret owners prefer a wire-bottomed cage with a removable bottom tray that catches droppings. Other ferret owners find that a ferret's droppings are not always confined by the edges of the tray and recommend using a high-sided litter box placed inside a trayless cage.

Whichever type of cage you choose, make sure its metal is nontoxic. And if you choose a cage with wire floors, keep in mind they are not user-friendly to tiny ferret feet. You'll want to add a sturdy, washable floor of some kind in the main living area. Linoleum or a strip of carpet are good choices, but indoor/outdoor carpeting, while washable, should be avoided because its thinner material can be chewed into pieces and swallowed.

If you are considering a multilevel cage, remember that ferrets, while fairly agile climbers, are not mountain goats. Have the ramps slope gently enough to allow easy ascent and descent. Also make sure that the upper stories are not so high that a ferret could get hurt if she fell.

Set up separate areas of the cage for eating, sleeping, and using the litter tray or box. Because ferrets may view food dishes as exciting new toys, you may want to use heavy ceramic bowls or dishes that attach securely to the cage.

Practically any small, shallow container makes a good ferret bed—an empty tissue box, sweatshirt sleeve, or even a plastic gallon milk jug with holes cut into it. Cardboard, while acceptable, will need to be changed frequently for hygiene and odor reasons. Avoid wicker, which can catch the toes of an unsuspecting ferret. There are also a variety of adorable sleeping hammocks, sleep socks, and beds on the market. One advantage to hanging beds is that they leave more cage space for playing.

Above: *Ferrets like to burrow, snuggle, and hide. A variety of cage components will keep your pet happily occupied.*
Left: *Cages should be set up so that they have separate eating, sleeping, and litter areas.*

Clean, old cotton T-shirts and other rags make good bedding. Be sure you remove any attachments such as hooks, buttons, and zippers that your ferret may swallow, and watch for signs that your ferret may be eating the material. Replace any shredded bedding material to prevent the ferret's nails from getting snagged. Some experts recommend avoiding terry cloth towels for the same reason. Do not use cedar chips, sawdust, or newspaper as bedding. In addition to being messy and odor absorbent, cedar chips are thought to cause respiratory problems in ferrets, and sawdust may irritate their eyes. Newspaper ink will get your ferret's fur dirty, and some experts say it too can cause respiratory problems.

Place the cage in a location that gets plenty of natural light and fresh air but is out of direct sun or drafts. What's merely warm to you can be fatal to a ferret.

Give your ferret's cage a thorough cleaning at least once a week. You'll obviously need to remove the ferret from the cage (a travel carrier may come in handy for keeping her out of trouble temporarily), along with the bedding and other accessories. Scrub the cage with hot,

Keeping your ferret's cage clean will eliminate odors and help keep your pet healthy.

soapy water with a few drops of bleach or other disinfectant added to kill germs. Rinse the cage thoroughly and
allow it to dry completely before you reassemble it. Don't
forget to wash and sanitize water bottles and food dishes
as well (some are conveniently dishwasher safe).

Litter Box Options

When out of the cage, ferrets may select certain corners for their bathrooms. A corner litter box placed in these problem areas will prevent recurring messes.

Commercial litter boxes are made of plastic or metal
and come in many shapes and sizes. An ordinary cat litter box, plastic storage box, or even a plastic dishpan
make good litter boxes for ferrets. You may want to cut
down one side to about 2½ or 3 inches so your ferret can
get in and out easily. And because nearly anything can be
a toy to a ferret, you may need to secure the litter box to
the cage.

Litter boxes specially designed with ferrets in mind
are now available at your pet store. These have two or
three high sides plus a lower side for the entrance. The
high sides help prevent accidents when the ferret backs
up to the edge.

You can fill the box with certain cat litters that work
just fine for ferrets. To protect a ferret's delicate respiratory

system, however, you should look for litters that do not contain a significant amount of dust. In general, clay-based and scoopable litters tend to be dustier, although some of these products are now advertised as being 99 percent dust-free. Some people prefer pelleted litter to help control odor and mess.

Toys and Tubes

Many terrific toys are available at pet stores, but just about anything a ferret finds around the house qualifies as a toy. Your car keys, socks, and sneakers, among other items, are all fair game and may wind up stashed in your ferret's favorite hideaway.

Ferrets find toys in anything they can pick up, whether they are car keys, socks, or other pets' toys.

Unfortunately, one common cause of death in ferrets is swallowing pieces of plastic or rubber chewed off a beloved toy. Plastic can lodge in a ferret's intestine, creating a dangerous blockage called an impaction. While an impaction can be surgically removed if caught in time, the surgery is no fun for the ferret, not to mention very expensive for the owner. And, sadly, the ferret may die if the problem isn't discovered in time.

So a big word of warning: Don't leave sneakers or other unintended toys within a ferret's reach. Chewing on such common items as kitchen sponges, rubber gloves, baby bottle nipples, children's toys and dolls, foam ear plugs, and rubber bands can all have tragic consequences. Also avoid commercial pet toys made of chewable soft latex or sponge rubber and those with protruding parts that can be chewed or broken off.

Relatively safe ferret toys include Ping-Pong and golf balls, hard rubber and nylon toys, many cat toys and baby rattles, and even a simple paper bag. Hollow rubber squeak toys are popular but do deteriorate and should be used only when you are with your ferret. Be sure to replace any toy your ferret has chewed a hole in.

Ferrets seem irresistibly drawn to anything that resem-

Toy Dos & Don'ts

- Do supervise playtime carefully.

- Do make sure that tubes and large balls are adequately ventilated.

- Don't give your ferret toys that can be chewed into pieces and swallowed.

- Don't leave toys inside the cage when you're not supervising playtime.

- Don't leave unintentional toys within a ferret's reach.

- Don't underestimate a ferret's ability to find what she shouldn't have.

bles a tunnel. Colorful clear plastic tubes that can be assembled in a variety of patterns are available at your pet store. Or you can make your own ferret tunnels using standard 3-inch plastic plumbing pipes. A large cardboard mailing tube or even the legs of old blue jeans (no zippers, rivets, or buttons, please) also work just fine. Always be on the safe side by supervising ferret playtime, and don't leave toys loose inside the cage.

Food and Water

Like many small animals, ferrets have a high metabolism. Their heart beats about three times a second, and food passes through their short digestive tract in about three to four hours. So it's no surprise that ferrets tend to eat frequent meals throughout the day. Thanks in part to the ferret's metabolism, obesity is rarely a problem. You may notice, however, that your ferret puts on a little weight in the wintertime.

Ferrets are carnivores. They need a diet high in animal protein,

A well-balanced ferret diet consists mostly of meat, fat, and protein. Avoid feeding ferrets a lot of grains and vegetables that are high in fiber, since ferrets don't digest fiber well.

but they also require a diet high in fat. Probably the best basic food for your ferret is specially formulated ferret food. But just because it says *ferret* on the bag doesn't mean you should buy the product without checking its ingredients. While studies have not yet definitively established the ferret's nutritional requirements, ferret experts suggest you make sure that the product contains between 32 and 40 percent animal protein and from 20 to 30 percent fat.

You may also feed your ferret a premium dry cat food. Because ferrets cannot assimilate plant protein, make sure the product contains animal protein. Some ferret owners like to feed dry kitten food to ferrets under the age of three, because it has a higher fat content than most adult cat foods. If you choose to feed your young ferret kitten food, be sure to switch over to adult cat food as your ferret ages. Too much protein in the diet has been associated with kidney problems in older ferrets. *Do not* feed dog food to a ferret.

Even though they may cost a little more, premium foods are a better choice because they tend to have a lower ash and corn content, ingredients linked to bladder stones and other problems in ferrets. Some ferret owners mix several brands of foods to try to ensure nutritional balance and provide a little variety. Others feel that mixing brands is not necessary if you're using a high-quality food formulated for ferrets.

Some experts believe one serving of canned cat food is permissible every one to two days to supplement the basic dry diet. Others feel a diet of strictly dry food is better for a ferret's teeth and gums. Whether or not you opt to supplement your ferret's diet with canned food, be sure that dry food is available continuously throughout the day. To prevent the growth of bacteria and to reduce odors, any leftover canned food should be removed immediately after mealtime.

Cooked eggs and fresh fruits and vegetables given in small amounts can supplement a healthy diet.

You can supplement your ferret's diet with small quantities of cooked meat, eggs, fruit, and vegetables. Just remember that such treats should be given sparingly—a teaspoon or so a day. While ferrets may love a taste of melon, banana, raisin, broccoli, or other fruits and vegetables, they do not have a cecum, a portion of the large intestine, and therefore they don't digest fiber well. Treats don't have to be human food. Some manufacturers now make semi-moist, meat-flavored treats especially for ferrets. Don't be surprised if you discover that your ferret has hidden little pieces of her favorite food under the sofa or inside her cage. Caching food is the ferret's way of saving for a rainy day.

Polecats and other undomesticated relatives of the ferret eat birds, frogs, mice, and other small animals. But for many reasons, including the potential for disease, it is not a good idea to feed those things to your ferret at home.

Do not give sweets, particularly chocolate, to your ferret either, even though she may beg for a taste. Refined sugars can damage a ferret's pancreas, which can result in diabetes or insulinoma later in her life. Chocolate may be something of a dietary staple for many humans, but it is toxic to ferrets.

Also, do not give milk products to your ferret, as they can cause diarrhea. Other dietary no-no's include chicken and turkey bones, which can splinter; dog food, which is high in ash and too low in protein; and anything salty.

A ferret should have fresh water available at all times—both in the cage and when she's out. Be sure to change the

An open drawer can be a ferret's play-ground and storage unit. Ferrets hide food and treats for a rainy day.

water daily. For the cage, a water bottle (the type made for small animals) attached to the outside often works best. A bowl is okay for either in the cage or outside use, but make certain the bowl is heavy enough that your ferret's energetic antics can't tip it over. Some ferrets have great fun playing in their water.

Above: *If your ferret prefers a water bowl, purchase a heavy ceramic one that cannot be tipped over.*
Below: *A water bottle may be a better choice than a water bowl, since it's less likely to get the cage wet.*

Supplements

Many people feel that if a ferret is fed a proper diet, vitamin and mineral supplements are not necessary or advisable unless prescribed by your veterinarian for a specific condition. Just as in humans, large doses of some vitamins may be toxic to ferrets.

Ferrets may need extra fat, however, during the cold winter months. If your ferret's coat appears thin and dry, ask your veterinarian about supplementing her diet with fatty acids such as Ferretone, Linatone, or Nutrical. There are a number of good products available at your pet store. Be sure to follow the label directions.

Ferrets love the taste of some of these fatty acid supplements so much that they can be useful in small amounts to facilitate nail clipping and other such endeavors. But don't overdo it. These supplements also contain vitamins A and D, so giving them as a routine snack could result in nutritional imbalances.

Living with Your Ferret

4

Before you bring your new ferret home, have things ready. Planning ahead will reduce stress on all concerned. In addition to a cage and litter box, make sure you have food supplies and a water bottle ready to go. Now is also the time to ferret proof your house!

Ferret Proofing to Avoid Common Hazards

Ferrets have an uncanny ability to find and get into places they shouldn't be. So before you introduce a ferret to your home (or any new place), put your brain in ferret mode. It may help to get down on your hands and knees to the ferret's eye level as you try to anticipate any potential trouble spots.

Ferrets can get into a lot of trouble around rugs, chairs, and cushions. Throw rugs and laundry piles make great spots for ferrets to burrow and hide in. Look before you step—and before you throw that heap of laundry into the washer.

Ferrets can and will get into trouble. Check for ferrets before running the dryer and other appliances.

A ferret can squeeze through the tiniest of spaces and will explore every aspect of his new environment. Any opening a ferret's head can fit through is big enough for the rest of his body to follow.

Always check before closing the refrigerator door when there's a ferret underfoot.

Although most ferrets won't sharpen their claws on upholstery the way cats sometimes do, ferrets will burrow beneath cushions, scout out any openings under the furniture, and even chew foam rubber padding (which can block the intestines) to make a nice little nest for themselves. When there's a ferret loose, don't sit down without looking for lumps in the cushions!

Reclining chairs and foldaway sofa beds can be particularly dangerous items around ferrets. They can get stuck inside the furniture or be seriously injured by its mechanism. Never move a mechanical piece of furniture without checking to be sure you know where your ferret is.

Ferrets are built for tunneling, so it's little wonder that they love to explore. Once they get into something, though, it can be hard to get them out. And sometimes they find escape routes to the great outdoors and get themselves into real trouble.

Look for any cracks (under doors, for example) more than about ¾ inch high or holes an inch in diameter or more. Any opening a ferret can get his head through is big enough for the rest of his body to follow. Typical trouble spots include spaces around plumbing pipes (under the sink, for example), dryer vent openings, cold-air returns, heating vent grates, and gaps around windows or screens. You'll also want to block off gaps under and around the dishwasher, stove, refrigerator, washer, and dryer if your ferret plays nearby.

Be careful your curious ferret doesn't sneak into an open refrigerator while you're rummaging inside for something.

And don't forget to inspect the inside of the dishwasher, washer, and dryer before starting them up!

Some ferrets find electrical wires, telephone cords, or even electric fans fascinating toys. Be sure to keep all cords and moving appliances out of your ferret's reach. Applying a bitter-tasting training spray or cream (like Grannick's Bitter Apple), which you can get at a pet store, to these hazards may help keep your ferret away from danger if one or two items seem particularly attractive.

Lock up household cleaners, which can be toxic to your ferret, and cleaning tools such as sponges and rags, which can cause intestinal blockage if chewed and swallowed.

Think carefully about what you keep under your sink or in lower cabinets and drawers. Many household cleansers are toxic to ferrets, and sponges can be deadly if chewed and swallowed. If you have no other good spot to store such items, latching your cupboard doors is a must. And remember: other items such as sneakers, rubber bands, cotton balls, and many children's toys can also cause intestinal blockage.

Ferrets enjoy getting into household plants too. Potting soil makes a lovely sandbox. To preserve your favorite houseplants, and your temper, keep plants away from ferrets. Some plants are also poisonous to animals. Keep your ferret away from azaleas, daffodils, dieffenbachia, ivy, mistletoe, oleander, and philodendron, to name a few. Tobacco and marijuana can also be harmful.

Introducing Your Ferret to His New Home

Keep sessions short when introducing your pet to his new home and family members.

The day you bring your new ferret home, chances are everyone in the household (plus a fair number of friends and neighbors) will be eager to meet the new arrival. But resist the urge to show off your pet right away. The ferret will be confused and disoriented by this major change in his life and routine. Give him a chance to rest and get used to his new surroundings.

Your ferret's first reaction may be to inspect his cage and perhaps look for a place to hide. You can't blame your ferret for being bewildered and a little scared. He will be much more interested in coming out to play after having some time to himself, some refreshment, and a nap. As the ferret starts to settle into his new home, you may find that he rearranges anything that's not fastened down, including the litter box, to suit his own tastes.

There are a few ways to acquaint your ferret to playtime outside of his cage. Most ferrets relieve themselves soon after they wake up, so remember to let your ferret do his business in the cage before you take him out to play. When you do take your ferret out, begin with short sessions. Make it a point to show any children in your household how to hold a ferret, with gentle support for both his forelegs and lower body. Emphasize that a ferret should never be picked up by his tail.

If you have other pets, introduce the ferret to them slowly and cautiously. Don't expect them to accept each other right away. Be prepared to intervene in case one of the animals becomes agitated or aggressive. To minimize friction, watch for territory infringement such as food raids. Although you'll want to pay particular attention during the getting-acquainted period, always supervise children and pets when a ferret is around.

Understandably, friends and neighbors may find your new pet fascinating. But think hard before you let people outside your immediate household come within biting range of even the most sweet-tempered ferret. That advice may sound harsh. The cold reality is that in many parts of

Watch out for territory disputes between ferrets and other pets. This ferret is trying to steal his cat roommate's food.

the country, even a simple nip reported to animal control authorities can result in your ferret being killed and tested for rabies, even if the ferret has been vaccinated with an approved rabies vaccine. For your ferret's sake, it's best to play it safe with a look-but-don't-touch policy.

In the excitement of bringing your new pet home, don't forget to make that first vet appointment. A thorough checkup will help ensure that your ferret gets off to a good start and will give your veterinarian baseline data for future reference. Be sure to schedule the appointment within any warranty period specified by your sales contract.

What to Expect

Creature comforts: an open clothes drawer makes a luxurious hideaway for a ferret who enjoys crawling into openings and hiding in small places.

Ferrets are curious, playful creatures. They are excellent problem solvers, especially when solving the problem means getting into places they aren't supposed to be.

Ferrets have keen senses of smell and hearing but relatively poor eyesight, especially in bright light. Avoid swooping down quickly from above to pick up a ferret, as he may not immediately recognize you as a friend. Approach your ferret slowly and speak softly so he will recognize you.

Ferrets have a lot of energy for exploring and will want

to visit and get acquainted with everything in a room before settling in to play or be sociable. Young ferrets are particularly energetic. Although they tend to settle down a little when they reach the age of six months or so, ferrets never really lose their playful ways.

Perhaps because they are so active when they are wide awake, ferrets sleep sixteen to twenty hours a day. Some people believe ferrets are nocturnal animals like their wild relative the polecat. As a practical matter, however, ferrets seem to make it a point to be awake at the times you are available to play with them.

Communication

Ferrets may not be able to talk, but you'll quickly learn to interpret their sounds and body language. One of the most striking of ferret behaviors is what is commonly called the weasel war dance—a twisting, tumbling dance of pure glee.

A ferret's tail can tell you a lot about what's going on in his head. Sometimes he twitches his tail like a cat in anticipation of some special treat. When the ferret is scared or very excited, he may puff out his tail till it resembles a bottle brush.

The weasel war dance is a celebration of life and an expression of pure glee.

Although ferrets are not generally noisy animals, you will find that they make a range of sounds to express curiosity, happiness, fear, and pain. Many vocalizations are variations of one basic ferret sound, often described as a "cluck" or "dook."

Ferrets often cluck when playing. Like dogs, ferrets may beg you to come and play with them by jumping up against your leg and then running away again, clucking encouragement at you all the while. A slow, soft clucking may mean the ferret is hot on the trail of something he is looking for. Faster clucking may signal excitement or anger.

A frightened ferret may hiss or bark—his way of issuing a warning to stay away. When play gets too rough, the ferret will squeal to let you know that he wants to be left alone. If the ferret is injured, he will scream.

Focus on Grooming

Ferrets have several grooming requirements, including nail clipping, bathing, brushing, and dental care.

A ferret's nails grow surprisingly fast. Unfortunately, long, sharp nails can snag on carpeting, furniture, and bedding, not to mention the potential damage they can do to clothing and tender skin! Because a ferret may actually pull a nail out in a frantic struggle to free himself, it is important to keep nails neat and trim.

Make it a habit to trim your ferret's nails regularly—

Nails grow quickly and should be clipped every one to two weeks.

every one to two weeks. Assemble your tools before you start. Nail clippers made for either cats or humans work just fine. Make sure you have styptic powder (available at your local pet store) on hand in case you should cut a little too close to the quick. In an emergency, you can use flour, cornstarch, or even bar soap to help stop bleeding, but it's better to keep styptic powder on hand.

As you can imagine, ferrets see no reason at all to sit still to have their nails trimmed. For these and other occasions when you need to control or immobilize the ferret (bath time, for example), "scruff" him. You scruff a ferret by holding him in one hand by the loose skin at the scruff of the neck, much the way a mother cat carries a kitten. Again, be sure to support the ferret's lower body. Let his weight rest in your lap or on a countertop, and have him facing away from you. Then rub a little Ferretone, Linatone, Nutrical, or a favorite treat on your ferret's belly to distract him. (Remember, don't overdo it, otherwise you may upset your ferret's nutritional balance.) Once your ferret is thoroughly engrossed in licking off the treat, you can clip away, usually without hindrance. In the case of a particularly stubborn little cuss, you may need to enlist a helper to scruff the ferret, holding him still while you work.

The part of the nail you want to cut is only the overgrowth; be careful not to clip back into the vein at the base of the nail. Look closely to find the pinkish vein before you start cutting. If your ferret has very dark nails, you may want to make several smaller snips rather than one big one to be sure you are not cutting too far. Angle your clippers so you do not accidentally snip a toe pad in the process. If you're a little nervous about the whole procedure, ask your vet, someone at your pet store, or breeder to coach you the first time. Some people prefer to clip their ferret's nails right after a bath, because the nails are a little softer.

Scruffing can be used to restrict your ferret's movements.

Right: Bathing your ferret will keep him healthy and sweeter smelling.
Below: Wet ferrets enjoy wiggling through towels to dry themselves.

Bathing your ferret regularly will help control odors and keep your ferret healthy. Be sure to plan ahead to allow enough time for the entire procedure, including time for drying off and playing. Some ferrets take to water. If you're lucky, your ferret will enjoy bathing enough to join you in the shower. But many ferrets squirm, wriggle, and generally do their best to avoid bath time.

Special shampoos designed for use on ferrets are now on the market. In a pinch, though, you can use a no-tears baby shampoo or a kitten shampoo. Most dog and even some cat shampoos can be too harsh for ferrets.

A kitchen sink with a sprayer attachment is handy equipment for a ferret bath. A bathtub works just fine too, but it's harder on your back. If you don't have a sprayer attachment on your sink, fill a sink or small tub with 2 to 3 inches of warm (not hot) water before you capture your bather. You may want to fill an unbreakable pitcher or other container with enough warm water for rinsing.

Holding your ferret firmly by the scruff of the neck, wet him gently, being careful not to get water up his nose. Then lather with the shampoo, being sure to include the ferret's head. Rinse off all the soapsuds, again taking care to keep water out of the ferret's nose. You may want to apply a coat conditioner, especially during winter months or whenever the air is dry.

Gently squeeze as much excess water from your ferret's fur as possible before putting him down, but don't worry about getting it all. Your ferret will dry himself if you simply lay a couple of towels on the floor for him to burrow in—and he'll have a good time doing it! Be sure the area is free of drafts and safely ferret proofed because ferrets also love to run around after a bath to get dry. A bath seems to make many ferrets extra frisky. Wait until he is completely dry before you put him back in his cage.

While overbathing can strip the oils from a ferret's fur and skin, one bath a week during summer and one every two weeks in winter will keep a ferret clean, shiny, and sweeter smelling.

It's important to keep your ferret's ears clean too. Some veterinarians say that normal earwax is protective,

It might be easier to clean ears after bathing your ferret. A healthy ferret's earwax is reddish brown.

Hold your ferret firmly when cleaning his ears to prevent him from making sudden movements and damaging the delicate eardrum.

Regular brushing will reduce hair balls and shedding.

so there is no need to clean all the wax out of your ferret's ears. However, if you want to clean your ferret's outer ears, bath time usually provides a good opportunity. Use a cotton swab and an ear-cleaning solution, which your veterinarian can prescribe. In a pinch, standard 3-percent hydrogen peroxide solution will work. Hold your ferret's head firmly by the scruff for this procedure, and don't attempt to clean the inside of the ear canal. One sudden shake of his head could result in damage to the ferret's delicate eardrum.

Like dogs and cats, ferrets can get ear mites and ear infections. Symptoms of a problem may include frequent ear scratching; any abnormal-looking discharge; or a black, waxy buildup. Normally, a ferret's earwax is reddish brown. If you suspect mites or an infection, check with your vet for a firm diagnosis. The vet may suggest using an over-the-counter cat medication or a prescription, depending on what the problem is.

In addition to bathing your ferret, you will also need to groom him. Not all ferrets take to grooming, though. As an

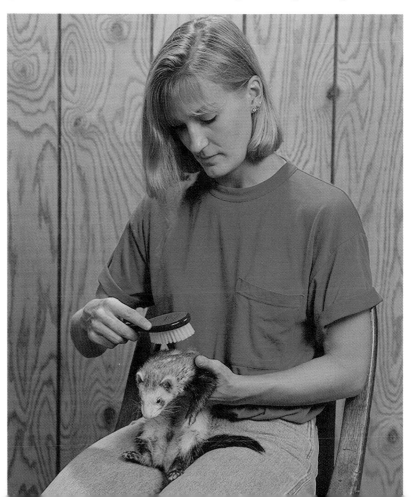

alternative, some experts recommend finger-grooming or plucking, especially during the molting season.

Ferrets change their coat (molt) twice a year. As winter approaches, you'll notice your ferret shedding his light summer coat. The guard hairs and underfur will get thicker and heavier—even if you happen to live in Florida. And you'll know it's spring when you find excess winter fur on his bedding.

Regular brushing can help reduce molting mess. At the height of molting season, you'll want to change your ferret's bedding more frequently. Instead of washing the bedding as usual, some people find it simpler just to throw it away at this time of year. Scout local garage sales and stock up on inexpensive T-shirts and sweatshirts to use as replacements.

A variety of ferret care products are available to make life with a ferret easier and more enjoyable.

While grooming your ferret, pay attention to changes in his coat and skin. Hair loss outside of molting season, excessive dryness, scratching, or any unusual lumps, bumps, or skin eruptions may signal a medical condition that your vet should know about.

For simple dry skin problems, though, try using a humidifier in the ferret's room. A conditioner at bath time and fatty acid supplements also may help. Some ferrets may be allergic to scented laundry detergents, so try switching to an unscented brand if you suspect that may be part of the problem.

Use a fine-toothed flea comb to test your ferret for fleas.

If your ferret goes outside or you have other pets who do, you'll want to watch for signs of fleas, particularly excessive scratching. To test for fleas, groom the ferret with a flea comb over a white towel or piece of paper. If your ferret has fleas, the flea dirt will appear against the whiteness as little black specks that turn red if moistened with water.

Most ferrets can be treated safely with an over-the-counter flea powder or shampoo made for kittens. Look for products that use relatively gentle ingredients such as natural or synthetic pyrethrins or insect growth inhibitors as their active ingredient. Avoid products made for dogs and any products that contain organophosphates.

Many ferret fanciers do not recommend flea dips, as their harsher chemicals may irritate a ferret's skin and could potentially be toxic to ferrets. Flea collars, too, are not a wise idea for ferrets, because they can get them off and may chew and ingest the chemically treated material.

From natural remedies to shampoos and powders to oral medications, many flea removal products will help combat those pesky parasites.

Some veterinarians report that the monthly oral flea product called Program is being used safely and effectively with ferrets. This product is available only from veterinarians, however, and has not been specifically tested and approved for use on ferrets. Ask your veterinarian to recommend a flea product before treating any ferret under three months old.

Just treating the ferret for fleas is not enough. To break the flea's life cycle, you need to rid the ferret's entire environment, including his cage, house, yard, and carrier, of immature fleas. Repeated applications of flea products are often needed. Be sure to read and follow label instructions. Some people report good results with products with the active ingredient boric acid, a natural compound that desiccates the flea and has a high margin of safety for pets and humans.

For particularly nasty flea infestations or if your own efforts just don't seem to be producing adequate results, it may be time to call in a professional exterminator. If you do decide to hire an exterminator, however, be sure to tell the company that you have a ferret, and insist that the technician apply only chemicals that are safe for ferrets.

Ticks are another pest that may consider your ferret an attractive host. If you find a tick on your ferret, clean the area around the tick using a cotton ball soaked with rubbing alcohol. With a pair of tweezers, grip the tick as close to the ferret's skin as possible and pull gently and firmly, but not quickly. The object is to remove the head of the tick, which is buried beneath the skin, along with the body. If the tick's body breaks off, leaving its head imbedded in your ferret's skin, it's best to take him to the veterinarian to have the tick's head removed. If you are successful at removing the tick, dab the site with peroxide or rubbing alcohol, then apply an antibiotic cream. Check the area during the next few days to be sure it doesn't become infected.

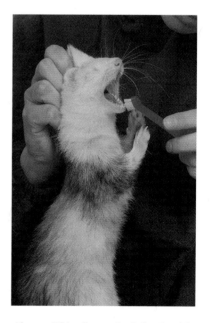

Ticks burrow into skin to feed on blood.

Just like your own teeth, a ferret's teeth (all forty of them!) should be cleaned periodically to remove built-up tartar and prevent gum problems. During your ferret's annual checkup, ask your vet to take a look at his teeth to see if they need cleaning. The ferret may need to be anesthetized while the cleaning is being done.

Older ferrets, particularly those kept on soft diets, sometimes develop tooth and gum problems. Symptoms may include obvious discomfort while chewing, or picking up and dropping food. You may need to moisten hard food a little to help the ferret eat until you can get him to the vet. Don't postpone needed dental work. Dental infections can lead to serious health problems, including kidney, liver, and heart disease. Feeding dry food to younger ferrets may help avoid these problems.

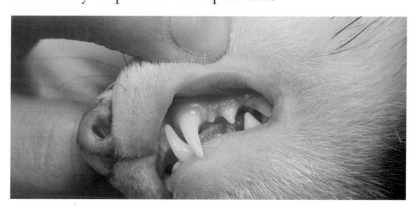

Above: *This silver mitt is having his teeth brushed.*
Left: *A vet should examine your ferret's teeth during his annual checkup.*

Training Your Ferret

5

Behavior Training

Teaching your ferret proper behavior is much like trying to keep a willful two-year-old child out of mischief—both require a generous measure of persistence and patience. Behavior training is important to ensure a well-mannered companion and to deter nipping and squirming. And training your ferret to use the litter box has its own obvious advantages.

Baby ferrets play rather rough-and-tumble games with each other. Luckily for them, ferrets' tough skin can withstand a good bit of playful nipping. Unfortunately for their human companions, however, kits may also find the earlobes and lips of their favorite people attractive targets. Some ferrets think our toes and feet make great mock prey too. While it may start out as hilarious fun, this can be a

Wrestling and nipping are parts of normal play behavior between ferrets.

tough game to end. Don't let your ferret get started as a toe chaser or ear nipper. It's important to teach your ferret what your limits are.

If nipping is a problem, some basic behavior modification techniques can help. Let your ferret know immediately when he bites too hard. A firm "no" or "bad" usually gets the message across. If the ferret bites and hangs on, grab him gently but firmly by the scruff of the neck. This reinforces your order and will usually get him to relax. You may find that a bitter-tasting training spray helps discourage biting behavior. Spray it on your own hands and feet or, if necessary, on another pet's neck.

Even though your patience may be tested, especially with a kit, remember just how much bigger you are than this little rascal. *Never* hit or swat your ferret. If you're not successful at reducing or eliminating nipping behavior on your own, consider enlisting the aid of an experienced ferret handler or an animal behavior expert. You should not have the ferret's teeth filed down.

Remember that nipping or biting can have fatal consequences for your ferret if someone reports an incident to animal control—even when your ferret has been vaccinated with a USDA-approved rabies vaccine. To avoid the risk of your ferret becoming a bite-case statistic, limit his contact with people until you are sure he's learned not to nip.

It's important to teach your ferret not to bite.

Consistently, firmly, and gently discipline your ferret. Never hit a ferret.

Consistently, firmly, and gently discipline your ferret. Never hit a ferret.

But that's not the only lesson a newly adopted kit must learn. Polite society sometimes requires that we sit still in certain circumstances, such as at weddings, in school, at the doctor's office, or when a special relative visits. Even though you may not want to have your ferret with you at such times, there will be similar occasions when you need your ferret to behave himself and sit quietly. Yes, it's asking rather a lot for an animal who loves frolicking so much to sit quietly. But he can and will learn. The keys to success are to start training early and to be consistent.

Begin by establishing some ground rules when you're holding the ferret. He will let you know in a flash when he wants to get down. Your job (and a tough one it can be) is to stand firm and let him down only when *you* want to put him down. Just like a human two year old, if your ferret learns that squirming, wiggling, and making a general pest of himself gets him what he wants, you'll see more of that annoying behavior. It's important to recognize that sometimes the ferret is squirming because it's time for a litter box break. Obviously, that's a signal worth heeding.

Scruffing the ferret, using a harness for gentle restraint,

Training Tips

- Speak softly to your ferret before you pick him up.

- Start early in your relationship to teach your ferret acceptable behavior.

- Use one word consistently when you want your ferret to stop misbehaving.

- Use a squeaky toy or other noisemaker each time you give a special treat.

- Remember, don't let your ferret train you (and he will try).

and reminding him verbally to stay (even if you begin to feel like a broken record) are all training methods that will help. You're making progress when the ferret relaxes and sits quietly; that's the time to treat your ferret lavishly. Rewards work far better with ferrets than punishment.

Many owners recommend using a squeaky toy, whistle, or rattle every time you get your ferret out of his cage or give him a treat so that he will associate the noise with a reward. Training your ferret to come in response to a special sound may pay important dividends if he should ever escape, or if he's simply prone to finding hiding places inside the house.

As time goes by, you'll find that it takes less and less time for your ferret to understand what behavior you expect. Just be sure that you are consistent in training the ferret; don't let your ferret train you!

Litter Box Training

There's good news and bad news when it comes to litter box training a ferret. The good news is that ferrets are naturally fastidious creatures. Once they have identified a certain spot as a toilet area, they tend to use the same place repeatedly. The bad news, however, is that ferrets often pick a place close at hand for a brand new bathroom rather than take the trouble to search out the old one. Most (but unfortunately not all) ferrets can be

Placing the ferret in his litter box after he wakes up will reinforce the proper place to go.

Keep litter boxes full of clean, dust-free litter to ensure proper use, good health, and odor reduction. Unlike cats, ferrets do not have the instinct to bury their wastes.

trained to use a litter box a good percentage of the time. But it will take some work, patience, and reinforcement on your part.

Start by training the ferret to use the litter box in his cage. Make sure you use a litter box with a low opening so the ferret can easily get in and out. Add some ferret feces to the litter to show your ferret that it's not a playpen.

You will notice that your ferret typically relieves himself promptly after waking up. If need be, you can help him figure out the proper use for the litter box by placing him there right after nap time and keeping him there until he does his business. Lavish praise and a treat for a job well done also may help. Because ferrets don't like to soil their living quarters, most ferrets will figure out how to use the litter box in their cage fairly quickly.

Training a ferret to use proper bathroom etiquette outside the cage can be a bit more difficult, however. Don't overwhelm him by giving him the run of the entire house all at once. Start with one small room or area—a bathroom

Ferrets prefer to eliminate in corners and tend to aim high, so a high-sided, corner litter box is a good, space-saving option.

or closed kitchen, for instance. Use a litter box similar to the one in the cage, place it in a convenient corner, and season it with some feces. Show the ferret where the litter box is by placing him in the box the first few times he visits the new room.

Some people advise ferret owners to allow their ferret to choose a corner of the room first, then place the litter box in that corner. But even that may not ensure continued success. Your best bet is to keep a close eye on your ferret and try to anticipate his actions, so that proper habits will be formed.

Once your ferret is successfully litter box trained in one room, gradually expand the area available to him. Be sure a litter box is conveniently placed in each room so your ferret doesn't have to search very far to find one.

Keep in mind that you attach far more importance to the litter box than your ferret does. As far as ferrets are concerned, if it's a corner, it will work just fine. So until your ferret is using the litter box habitually, you'll need to watch him carefully. If you see his tail begin to go up in some new corner of his own choosing, scoop him up quickly and put him in a litter box until he's done his business. You may even want to practice an ounce of prevention and place him in a litter box every hour or so, whether he shows the inclination or not.

Some ferrets have a higher aim than you may imagine. If you find that your ferret repeatedly is doing his business over the edge of the litter box, you'll need to find a box with higher sides. Some commercial litter boxes are now made with high backs especially for ferrets. Your local pet store should have one or be able to get one.

Ferrets may shun a litter box if it's not up to their standards of cleanliness, so you'll want to keep the litter boxes clean in self-defense. Even a basically well-intentioned ferret is going to make mistakes, especially if he's excited, upset, or his routine has been disturbed. If you catch him in the act, tell him "no" and put him promptly in the litter box. If you don't catch the culprit right away but find a mess later, don't bother trying to correct him. Ferrets do not associate their mistakes with reprimands that come more than a few seconds after the fact.

Don't get angry, and never punish the ferret for a litter box lapse. Just watch closer the next time so it doesn't get repeated. Clean up the mistake with a deodorizing disinfectant so the ferret won't be encouraged by the odor to use the same spot again.

Collars

The use of collars on ferrets is a bit controversial. Some people feel it's important to keep an identifying collar on a ferret at all times, just in case he should manage to escape. The collar can alert strangers that this unusual-looking animal is not wild, and can also give information to help get him safely home again. A collar with a bell on it can also alert you to your ferret's whereabouts—an important warning in case he's chosen to burrow in a stack of laundry or under a throw rug!

You will want to weigh the pros and cons when deciding whether to place a collar on your ferret.

Other ferret owners are convinced that a collar is useless at best and dangerous at worst. Ferrets can slip right out of many collars and could choke to death if a collar or tag gets caught on furniture or the cage.

If you decide to put a collar on your ferret, choose one that fits snugly enough not to get caught on furniture, but has an elastic band so the ferret can easily slip out in an emergency.

So there's the dilemma. If the collar is loose enough that the ferret can slip free easily, then choking is probably not much of a hazard—but the collar probably won't stay on long enough to do much good either. It's up to you to decide whether the benefits of a collar outweigh the risks.

If you do decide to use a collar, aim for a snug but not uncomfortably tight fit. Look for materials and designs that are not apt to get caught on furniture or cage parts. For example, one type of tag fits flush against the collar instead of dangling from it. Some collars also have an elastic strip, which makes it easier for ferrets to get them off in case of trouble but also easier for them to ditch. You might also decide to put a collar on your pet only while he is out of his cage.

Using a Harness and Leash

Walking a ferret is hardly the same experience as walking a dog. You may be able to train your ferret to tolerate a harness, but a busy ferret has far too many things to explore to want to walk in a straight line with you.

A harness and leash allows a curious ferret to safely venture out and explore the exciting world.

If you decide to take your ferret outside, however, a harness and leash are a good safety precaution. They allow the ferret room to explore within a limited area and also give you more control than if you tried to carry him in your arms. Safety is not the only consideration, however. Regulations in certain parts of the country, such as Michigan, may require that ferrets be either leashed or caged when away from home.

While you can use leashes and harnesses made for cats or other small animals, your best bet is to get one designed specifically for a ferret's proportions. As with a collar, the harness should be snug but not tight. Do not simply snap a leash directly onto a collar, as a determined ferret may be able to wriggle free.

This sable ferret is wearing a harness for the first time.

Training your ferret to accept a harness, like pretty much everything else, is mostly a matter of patience. Some ferrets adapt fairly quickly; others are never quite happy about the matter. You'll want to practice putting the harness on at home. Leave it on for only a few minutes at a time at first. After a few sessions with the harness alone, attach the leash and let your ferret adjust to the feel of that for a while. If you let your ferret run around the house with the leash trailing, watch carefully to make sure the leash doesn't get hooked on or tangled around anything.

Playtime and Tricks

Ferrets do need time outside their cages for play and exercise, but they don't need special exercise equipment. Left to their own devices, they get quite a workout just running around! Interactive toys can be fun for ferret and owner alike. You can also have hours of fun just watching as your ferret explores a maze of tunnels or a ball with holes cut for in-and-out play.

You can also teach your ferret some basic tricks. Younger ferrets often learn tricks more readily than older ferrets, but with consistency and patience, even older ferrets can learn to perform. Most ferrets will learn a trick in five or six sessions, but every ferret is different. Some take a little longer, some will learn one trick but not another, and some just seem determined to ignore your efforts entirely.

Tasty treats will help teach your ferret to sit up.

Ferrets have a short attention span and can fill up rather quickly on treats, so keep training sessions to about ten minutes at a time. For the quickest results, set time aside every day to repeat the lesson, and work on only one trick at a time until that trick is mastered before going on to the next.

To begin teaching your ferret to sit up, put a small dab of Ferretone or Linatone on your finger and let him lick it briefly. Raise your hand slowly above your ferret's head, repeating a command, such as "sit up." Gradually increase

Fun-loving ferrets can also learn tricks such as rolling over.

the distance until the ferret stands on command to get the treat.

To teach your ferret to roll over, give the command to roll over as you gently turn your ferret over by his shoulders. Reward him immediately with his favorite treat. After a few repetitions, give the roll-over command and roll your ferret only part of the way, letting him make the rest of the turn himself. Again, give a treat when he has completed the turn. With a little more prompting, your ferret will eventually learn to roll on the command alone. Some ferrets learn the trick so well they roll over as their way of saying "please" whenever they want something!

While most ferrets will readily learn to ride on your shoulder, a ferret may not pay close attention to maintaining his balance at first and can fall. Try to get the ferret used to your shoulder while you're sitting on the floor so the falling distance won't be so great. Graduate to moving around on your knees, and then to a standing position. Move slowly until the ferret gets used to hanging on. Eventually, your ferret will be able to ride on your shoulder while you walk at a normal pace. A hooded sweatshirt will give the ferret a more secure spot to ride.

The Great Escape–What to Do

It's a ferret owner's nightmare—you call, and your little darling doesn't come. What do you do? Don't panic. Ferrets are great at finding new places in the house to hide and sometimes just decide to catch a nap while they're there. They may very well show up for dinner within a few hours.

In the meantime, however, you don't want to take the chance that your ferret might be trapped or injured. Check

These problem-solving sable and silver mitt ferrets look like they are plotting their escape out into the world.

Microchips

Microchips are a relatively new way to identify pets, although they have been used for years to identify rare or expensive animals such as racehorses and zoo animals. Many animal shelters across the country now have scanners in place, and some local animal-control agencies are starting to require microchip identification as part of their licensing programs.

A microchip is a radio-wave-activated transponder encased in a tiny glass tube. The entire package is about the size and shape of a grain of rice. Using a special needle, a veterinarian inserts the microchip under an animal's skin, a process that takes mere seconds. No anesthesia is needed.

Once in place, the microchip is inert until activated by a radio signal from a compatible reader. The microchip then sends back to the reader a unique, precoded identification number, that can be matched to a number on a database to identify the owner.

Pet owners who choose to have their pets tagged with a microchip generally pay both the veterinarian's fee for implanting the microchip and a one-time registration fee to a database company. The company maintains a record of the pet's ownership and operates a recovery hot line. Microchip clinics offered through local veterinarians, animal control agencies, or pet stores sometimes provide the service at discounted rates.

Even though microchip technology is considered safe and effective, it's not a perfect solution to the lost pet problem. For the microchip to be detected, someone who finds an animal must take him to a vet or a shelter that has a scanner. In addition, some scanners are not accurate when reading other companies' chips. Previous problems with incompatible technologies among the various microchip companies soon should be a thing of the past, thanks to recent agreements to produce a universal scanner that will be able to read all manufacturers' chips. You can get further information on microchips from your veterinarian, local ferret club, or shelter.

his last known whereabouts carefully. Could he be burrowing in the furniture? Did you open any drawers he could have slipped into? Could he have sneaked into the refrigerator the last time you opened it?

If you suspect that your ferret may have escaped outdoors, investigate any ferret-enticing spots, such as holes, woodpiles and parked vehicles, nearby. If your ferret is trained to come to a special sound, make sure you have his favorite treat in hand and repeat your come-and-get-it command.

Scanners pick up identification codes from tiny microchips (below) inserted under the skin.

If that doesn't work, you'll want to pursue all the usual options for finding a lost pet in your community, such as putting up posters, contacting veterinarians and the local humane society or animal shelter, and placing an ad in the newspaper. In addition, notify your immediate neighbors to keep an eye out. Sometimes information can trickle in on the kid grapevine. Ask local children to let you know if anyone at school has found an unusual animal.

No form of pet identification is perfect, but the chances of your ferret being returned to you are greater if your pet has a secure collar with a tag and a microchip. All in all, it's cheap insurance. You might think about those options now, before disaster strikes.

Going Visiting

You may be dying to bring your ferret to show him off at school, to ferret shows, or even to visit friends. But a few cautions are in order.

Ferrets love new places and will be eager to explore every nook and cranny. Unfortunately, many places you may want to bring a ferret have not been ferret proofed. To avoid problems with unfamiliar situations, be sure your ferret is secured in either a portable cage or a harness with a leash so he can't wiggle free.

Go prepared. Whenever you take your ferret for a visit, make sure you bring along food, water, and a small litter box. Your friends, and your ferret, will appreciate it.

Be sure that the ferret will not be exposed to heat. Taking your ferret to a roasting Fourth of July picnic or for a day at the beach is not a good idea.

If your child wants to bring the ferret to school, make sure that it's okay with the teacher first. You will also need to consider whether the other children in the class will handle the ferret gently. It's a good idea for you to be present during any show-and-tell, both to monitor interaction with the ferret and to bring him home so he doesn't have to spend the entire day at school.

Ferret shows can be great fun, but remember—with a multitude of ferrets around, there is also the potential for illness being passed around. Early outbreaks of a highly

Ferrets are an interesting subject for show-and-tell.

Ferret shows can be great fun, particularly if your ferret wins a ribbon.

contagious diarrhea known as the green slime virus, for example, were reportedly traced to ferrets who had attended a particular show. Although show promoters go to great lengths to ensure that shows are fun, safe places to be, let caution be your guide. If your ferret has a cold or any symptoms of disease, *do not* bring him to a show.

At school, at shows, or whenever your ferret is around strangers, keep in mind that a ferret bite can lead to severe consequences. In some areas when a bite is reported, animal-control officers are under instructions to seize the ferret and have him killed and tested for rabies—even if he has been properly vaccinated. In other parts of the country, however, animal officials merely place the animal in quarantine. Be sure you know what the risks are where you live and visit.

Always be prepared when traveling with a ferret. Take along food, water, and a small litter box as well as a harness and spray bottle.

Vacations

Your Place or Mine?
Finding a Ferret Baby-Sitter

If you're going to be gone for more than a day, it's important to line up a reliable ferret baby-sitter. You may be lucky enough to have a friend or neighbor who would be tickled to ferret-sit, or there may be a neighborhood teenager who is good with animals and would like to earn a little extra money. While it's best if your baby-sitter has had some experience with ferrets, that perfect situation may not always be available. Above all, be sure your baby-sitter has a kind manner with animals and is extremely dependable.

Be sure to interview a few ferret-sitters before deciding on the one who's right for you.

Ferret-Sitter's Checklist

A checklist of basic information about your ferret is a helpful guide for your ferret-sitter.

- Name and phone number of your vet

- How to reach after-hours emergency veterinary care

- Your travel itinerary and phone numbers where you can be reached

- A backup emergency contact (preferably a local person) who can make decisions if you can't be reached

- Detailed written instructions about your ferret's food, water, and cage care

- Pertinent medical information about your ferret, such as instructions for giving medications and signs or symptoms to watch for

- A list of household dangers such as the cleansers under the sink and the houseplants

Ask your sitter to come over and spend some quality time with the ferret a few times before you leave so the two can get to know each other. These visits will also give your sitter a chance to ask questions he or she might not otherwise think of until after you are gone.

If you draw a blank among your network of friends and acquaintances, your veterinarian or local pet store may be able to recommend a boarding kennel or may be equipped to board animals themselves. Be sure to ask about the boarding costs and the bite policy. Request a tour of the facility ahead of time. Remember that if you leave your ferret anywhere that other animals are present, there is always the possibility she may be exposed to disease or parasites. Be sure the facility's standards are up to yours!

Another alternative is to hire a commercial pet-sitting service that comes to your home to take care of your pet. Pet-sitters often advertise in the yellow pages or in local newspapers. Because the sitter will be coming into your home, be sure the service is licensed, bonded, and insured. Find out how long the sitter has been in business, and ask for the phone numbers of previous clients as references. Ask about the sitter's bite policy, and be sure to pin down the total cost, including any additional fees, such as fees for giving medication.

If you hire a commercial pet-sitting service, expect to sign a contract spelling out your obligations and theirs, a form releasing the service from liability, and an authorization for veterinary treatment of your pet in case of emergency.

If your ferret is going to be cared for in someone else's home, make sure the area is properly ferret proofed. All too many ferrets who end up at shelters are there because they took advantage of their owner's absence to check out the world outside.

Traveling with Your Ferret

Traveling with your ferret takes some careful planning. Be sure you allow yourself plenty of time to make arrangements.

First and foremost, find out whether ferrets are legal in the areas you will be visiting and passing through. There may be special rules depending on how long you plan to stay. Call the Department of Agriculture or State Veterinarian of each state where you'll be traveling. National ferret organizations can help you obtain the names of local contacts to help you steer clear of cities or counties that don't allow ferrets. For international travel, be sure to ask both U.S. Customs and the foreign country's embassy for pet-related requirements and restrictions.

If you will be flying, it's a good idea to make your reservations early because there may be limits on the total number of pets the airline will accept per plane. Also, airlines sometimes put embargoes on pet travel during seasons when the animals might be exposed to extremely hot or cold temperatures.

Ask an airline representative about the regulations for transporting live animals. The airline may allow your ferret to fly in the cabin with you if she is confined in an approved travel carrier that fits under the seat. Other airlines allow ferrets to travel only in the cargo hold, which is temperature

While you're on the road, keep your ferret in a well-ventilated cage, taking care not to leave her in hot or drafty areas.

Whether traveling by car or plane, your ferret will be safest confined in her carrier.

controlled. Ask if you will need to present a health certificate before boarding. And don't forget to get the name of the person you speak with in case follow-up is needed.

If you are crossing state lines, you should have with you an interstate health certificate for small animals and a rabies/distemper vaccination certificate signed by your veterinarian. Different states have different requirements, but most require the health certificate to be dated within ten days of the travel date. That means if you are going to be away from home for more than ten days, you may need to get another health certificate from a local veterinarian before you return home.

Make sure that your planned accommodations are ferret friendly. Ask hotels about their pet policies before making reservations. And be sure that friends and relatives you will be staying with are prepared for both you and your companion.

It's safer for you and the ferret if you keep her confined to a travel cage during a car trip. If you're considering allowing your ferret some freedom, picture trying to brake for a stop sign—only to find her curled up under the pedals! Ferrets also have been known to carve out terrific little hideaways for themselves inside car upholstery.

Hot Weather Cautions

Considering those luxurious fur coats, it's not surprising that ferrets prefer cool weather. It's more than just a matter of taste, however. With only a few poorly developed sweat glands, ferrets can suffer serious injury, or even death, from heatstroke in temperatures above 85 degrees Fahrenheit. That means you should never leave your ferret closed up in a car or in direct sunlight on warm summer days. Older ferrets may be particularly sensitive to high temperatures.

Symptoms of heatstroke include panting, sluggishness, and bright red gums. In more extreme cases, the ferret becomes limp. If you suspect heatstroke, even if your ferret is still able to stand and walk, call your vet immediately. Proper treatment will involve gradually cooling her

Make sure your ferret gets plenty of fluids by carrying her water bottle with you on your journeys.

body using dampened towels or light spritzes of water. You can also apply a wet cloth to the ferret's soles and armpits. *Do not* immerse the ferret in cold water, apply ice, or otherwise cool her too rapidly. Your veterinarian may decide it is best for you to bring the ferret in for treatment or observation, even if she seems to be feeling better. Remember, heatstroke is a potentially life-threatening condition.

Plan ahead to avoid heatstroke when you travel with your ferret during the summertime. Make sure your car and its air conditioning are in good working order before you go. And even in moderately warm weather, don't travel unprepared.

Before leaving home, make a giant ice cube by freezing water in a self-sealing plastic bag or a plastic bottle. Don't forget to leave room for the water to expand before you put it in the freezer. Wrap the frozen bottle or bag with a non-terry towel so it's cool but not cold to the touch. Put it in the car where your ferret can find it to chill out if necessary. You can also fill a clean spray bottle with water to dampen her fur occasionally for a cooling effect.

Don't forget that heat can build up inside a parked car

To treat heatstroke, gradually cool your ferret by wiping her with a damp cloth or spritzing her with water.

Ferrets overheat easily. Since heat builds up quickly in a hot car, your best bet is to take your ferret with you, even if you're stopping for just a short while.

extremely quickly. A short stop for lunch can lead to disaster in warm weather. If necessary, skip the fine dining until you reach your destination and rely on fast-food drive thrus en route.

You will, of course, want to bring plenty of ferret food and water for the trip. Because water containers will slosh, you may need to take the water bowl or dispenser out of the cage while you are in motion. Do not let your ferret go for very long without stopping to offer her water.

Many people find that a space-saving, triangular litter box fits just perfectly in a travel cage. If necessary, season the new litter box with a bit of feces to give your ferret the right idea.

If there are three cardinal rules for traveling with your ferret, they are (1) always carry your veterinarian's phone number with you; (2) never let strangers, however well meaning, play with your ferret or put their fingers in her cage; and (3) don't let your ferret get overheated.

Bon voyage!

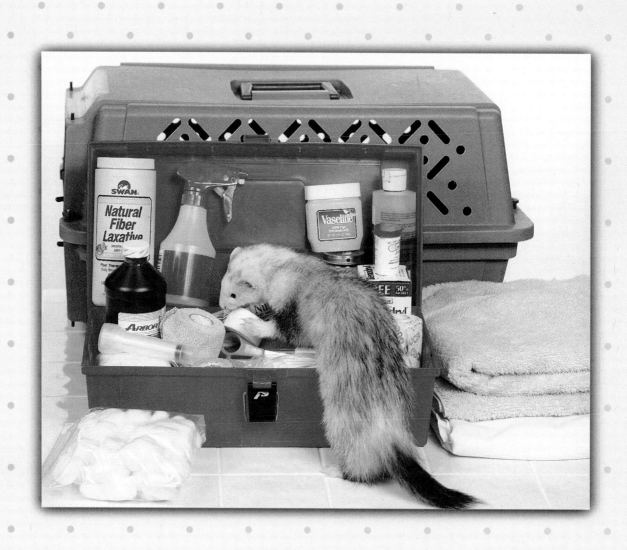

Medical Basics

I t's sad but true—ferrets are susceptible to a variety of illnesses and diseases. To keep your ferret in the very best of health, it is important to find a veterinarian who is good with ferrets and to schedule regular checkups.

Veterinarians often specialize in an area of medicine or group of species that interests them. A local pet shop, breeder, or ferret organization may be able to refer you to a veterinarian who is particularly knowledgeable about ferrets. If you can't find a referral, check the yellow pages and call some veterinarians to ask whether treating ferrets is a large, medium, or small part of their practice. If a veterinarian sees fewer than two or three ferrets a week, you may want to continue searching for a more ferret-intensive medical practice.

Don't be afraid to ask questions before making up your mind. When you call a prospective vet, ask what types of surgeries he or she has performed on ferrets and whether the clinic is equipped with Isoflurane, a very safe anesthesia for ferrets. Before bringing the ferret in for his first visit, always discuss the clinic's policy for cases in which a ferret may nip a staff member.

Emergencies don't always occur during normal business hours, and many vet emergency clinics do not know much about ferret medicine. So when you locate a ferret vet, be sure to ask how he or she handles emergencies at night or on weekends. Is someone on call at all times, or does the office simply refer you to a local emergency clinic? Is there a special number to dial, or a beeper procedure for after-hours help? Finding out about emergency procedures now may save you crucial minutes later.

It's also a good idea to call the emergency facility before an emergency comes up and ask the same questions you asked when choosing a vet, such as how many ferrets are seen there and what the bite policy is.

The following information is designed to help you know what to expect during a routine exam and to acquaint you with common ferret vaccinations and medical conditions. It is not intended to provide medical advice or to take the place of a consultation with your veterinarian. If you have any medical questions about your ferret or suspect any medical problem, always consult your vet.

Routine Checkups

Many veterinarians recommend that ferrets have a complete physical examination once a year until they are three years old, and twice a year after that. Of course, if your ferret develops a particular illness, more frequent visits may be necessary.

It may help to write down any questions you have for the vet before your appointment. Make note of important symptoms such as lethargy, itching, hair loss, vomiting, diarrhea, coughing, diminished stools, diminished appetite, a change in sleeping patterns, or difficult breathing. Be sure to bring to his or her attention any unusual lumps or behavioral changes in your ferret, even if they seem relatively minor.

If this is your ferret's first visit to a new vet, be sure to bring along his medical history, including information about the vaccinations your ferret has already had. If you don't know your ferret's medical history, bring the phone number of the place that sold you the ferret so your vet can call and find out.

During a physical exam, the veterinarian will check your ferret's eyes for any abnormalities or discharge; look in his ears for mites or infection; check the condition of his teeth

During your ferret's annual checkup, the veterinarian will listen to your ferret's heart and feel for any abnormal lumps or changes in his body.

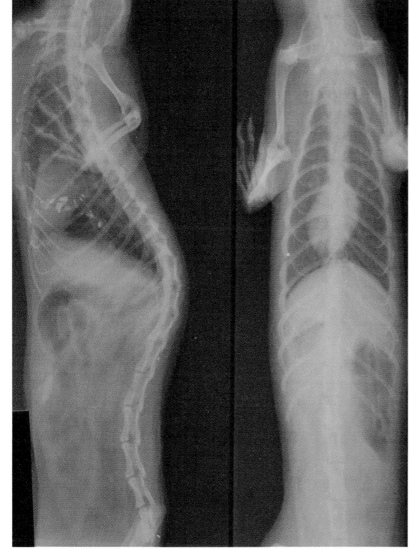

An annual, whole-body X ray is often recommended for the detection of tumors and diseases.

and gums; listen to his heart; inspect his fur and skin for fleas, ticks, lice, or skin tumors; and feel his abdomen, lymph node areas, and muscles for swelling or unusual lumps.

For ferrets over the age of three, veterinarians often recommend annual whole-body X rays to look for tumors, degenerative joint disease, and diseases of the heart and lungs. Although X rays are a fairly quick procedure, some ferrets need to be anesthetized to keep them still enough to take the pictures. Some vets also use ultrasound when heart disease is suspected or to help diagnose cases involving abdominal masses.

Your veterinarian also may recommend complete blood count (CBC), chemistry panel, and fasting blood-sugar tests annually for ferrets under age five, and twice a year thereafter. The CBC and chemistry panel are important screening devices to detect a variety of problems including lymphoma, a cancer of the lymph glands that many ferrets develop in later years. The blood sugar test can help diagnose insulinoma and kidney problems. Testing your ferret while he is still young will give your veterinarian baseline data to help detect abnormalities that may develop later in your ferret's life.

At each annual exam, your veterinarian may ask you to bring in a stool sample that he or she can check under the microscope for intestinal parasites such as roundworms, hookworms, coccidia, and *Giardia*.

Vaccinations

Ferrets need to be vaccinated routinely against rabies and distemper. Keeping your ferret's vaccinations current takes a little thought and organization. Try to schedule the next annual or semiannual visit before you leave your veterinarian's office, or put a note on your calendar to remind

Vaccinating your ferret against rabies and distemper is an important step in ensuring your ferret's safety and health.

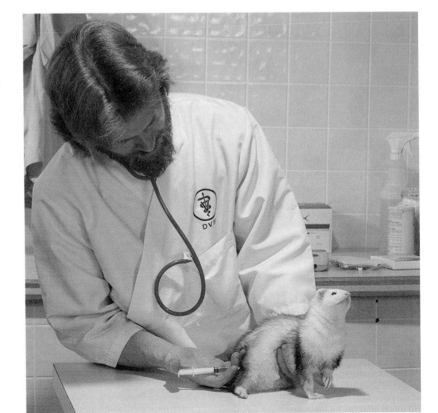

Rabies

Although only twelve confirmed cases of rabies in ferrets have been reported in the United States since 1957, and fewer than two dozen cases have been recorded during this century, there is a risk—however small—of ferrets contracting the rabies virus. The virus, found in the saliva of rabid animals, is spread through the bite of the infected animal. Rabies infection in ferrets is fatal—there is no treatment.

While the potential risk is extremely small, especially for ferrets kept indoors, the American Ferret Association, Inc., and many veterinarians recommend that you vaccinate your ferret against rabies anyway. State or local animal laws also may require that ferrets be vaccinated.

A rabies vaccination is a fairly routine procedure. Ferrets typically are vaccinated against rabies at twelve weeks of age, and booster shots are required each year thereafter. Of course, no vaccination or drug is entirely risk-free. Some ferrets do have an allergic reaction to the shot. As a precaution, plan to spend at least thirty minutes in your veterinarian's office after the vaccination to make sure your ferret does not develop any unusual symptoms. Adverse reactions may include itching, respiratory distress, hemorrhagic diarrhea, or shock. As a precaution, some ferret experts advise waiting two weeks after any other vaccination, such as distemper, before giving the rabies shot.

Many ferrets acquired from breeders already have had their initial rabies vaccination. To be on the safe side, however, be sure to ask for documentation before you bring your ferret home, and remember to mark your calendar for the annual booster shot. Baby ferrets from a pet store may be too young to have had their first rabies vaccination, but again, be sure to ask.

yourself to call to schedule the shots. Your veterinarian's office may send out reminder notices, but you may move, or the computer may hiccup, and the notice may never reach you. It's really up to you to keep track.

Keep records of your ferret's vaccinations in a place where you can find them readily. Although your veterinarian makes notes in your ferret's file, don't depend upon his or her record keeping. Your vet should provide you with a written certificate of each vaccination, either as part of your receipt or as a separate document. Keep these certificates handy. If your ferret should bite a person or another animal, it may be critically important to prove that your ferret's vaccinations are current.

At present, there is one rabies vaccine on the market (Imrab-3) that has been approved by the USDA for use in ferrets. Even with an approved vaccine, your ferret may still be at risk if he bites somebody. Research studies to determine the shed time (the time between exposure to the virus and when it appears in a ferret's saliva) for the rabies virus have not yet been completed. Some animal-control officials therefore believe that even a properly vaccinated ferret should be killed and tested for rabies if he bites a person. In other parts of the country, ferrets are quarantined to see if the disease develops. Completion of the shed time research is important to help set rational policy guidelines in this area.

In addition to rabies, ferrets can contract canine distemper. The distemper virus spreads through direct contact with an infected animal. It can also be carried on the clothes or hands of animal caretakers for at least eight hours. The virus can even be transmitted through the air for short distances. Unfortunately, this disease is considered untreatable in ferrets and almost invariably leads to a swift, painful, and all-too-avoidable death.

Initial distemper vaccinations are usually given in a

Heartworm

Your veterinarian knows it as dirofilariasis (from the scientific classification, *Dirofilaria immitis*), a parasite that lives inside the chambers of an animal's heart. Heartworm disease has been common for many years in the southern United States and is now showing up in other parts of the country as well. The heartworm is transmitted by mosquitoes. And because mosquitoes don't always stay outdoors, even indoor pets can be infected.

Symptoms of heartworm disease in ferrets include lethargy, abdominal fluid, coughing, or difficult breathing. Your veterinarian may also detect a heart murmur or increased bronchovesicular sounds in the ferret's lungs.

When a vet tests for heartworm disease, he or she checks the ferret's blood for either microfilaria (the immature stage of heartworm) circulating in the ferret's blood, or antigens produced by the host as a reaction to the adult heartworm. Unfortunately, it is common for both tests to yield false negative results. If the tests come back negative but your veterinarian still suspects a heartworm problem, X rays and ultrasound may come in handy as additional diagnostic techniques.

Heartworm disease can be difficult to treat successfully in ferrets. Although they tolerate the arsenic-based drug typically used to kill the parasite, ferrets are apt to develop potentially fatal blood clots. Some veterinarians have added anticlotting medication to the heartworm treatment to help combat this side effect. Once the parasitic worm has been killed, the ferret will still need up to three months of strict cage rest to regain his strength.

The good news is that heartworm prevention is cheap and easy to administer. Some veterinarians recommend heartworm preventive medication for ferrets beginning at the age of four months. If your ferret is over six months old, your vet may want to test him for heartworm before starting him on the medication. In areas where heartworm is endemic, your veterinarian may recommend medication year-round. In other areas, it may be necessary only during the warmer months of the year (typically April through October). If you have discontinued the medication, it's a good idea to bring your ferret in for a heartworm test before you start administering the medication again.

series of three shots. A ferret gets his first shot at the age of eight weeks and the two booster shots at the ages of eleven and fourteen weeks. If a ferret is over fourteen weeks old when the first shot is administered, a slightly different schedule may be recommended by your veterinarian. Once the initial series of distemper shots has been given, your ferret should have a booster annually.

Most ferrets purchased from pet shops or breeders have had only the first distemper shot. The whole series of shots is needed for ferrets to be properly immunized. Be sure to find out when you buy your pet exactly which distemper shots he has had, and mark your calendar to be sure the series is completed.

A veterinarian can reduce adverse reactions to the distemper vaccination by administering the injection in the rump, leg, or hip instead of the neck or shoulder.

Ferrets can have adverse reactions to the distemper vaccination, ranging from minor irritation and stinging at the injection site to vomiting and convulsions. Severe reactions are relatively rare. At least one study indicates that adverse reactions from the distemper vaccine may be significantly reduced if the veterinarian chooses your ferret's rump, leg, or hip as the injection site rather than the neck or shoulder. As with the rabies vaccine, it is a good idea to stay an extra half hour at the vet's after the vaccination and to watch your ferret closely for the next forty-eight hours or so, just to be sure there is no adverse reaction. Remember, to minimize the risk of adverse reactions, it's a good idea to schedule different vaccinations a week or two apart.

Most veterinarians believe ferrets are not susceptible to feline distemper, feline leukemia, or panleukopenia, and that vaccinations against those diseases are not necessary.

Ferret Ailments

Ferrets, like humans, can catch colds and the flu, and ferrets can catch these illnesses from humans. If you're not feeling well, avoid playing with your ferret so you don't pass the misery around. Germs can travel the other way, too. If your ferret has the sniffles, try not to snuggle with him for a few days, and wash your hands promptly after handling his food and water dishes.

A ferret with a cold or flu displays the same sort of symptoms as a human: drippy nose, lack of energy, congestion

The Green Slime Virus

The name sounds a little like something out of a 1950s grade-B science fiction movie, but the disease itself is nothing to laugh at. The green slime virus, more formally known as epizootic catarrhal enteritis of ferrets, or ECE, first made its appearance in the mid-Atlantic states in 1993 and has since spread widely across the United States.

The virus kills the cells that line a ferret's small intestine, leaving the ferret unable to absorb nutrients and water properly. The disease's signature symptom is severe, bright green diarrhea. The diarrhea is sometimes preceded by vomiting. This disease is highly contagious and can spread quickly through populations of ferrets housed together.

Although the green slime virus may be transmitted by contact with the saliva or feces of an infect-ed ferret, it may also be passed indirectly. Sick ferrets should be isolated and should not share food dishes, toys, or litter boxes with other ferrets. After touching an infected ferret, you should wash your hands and change clothes before handling a ferret who has not been exposed.

Ferrets infected with the green slime virus can experience rapid dehydration due to fluid loss, and in a small number of cases (fewer than 5 percent), the disease can lead to death within forty-eight hours. Older ferrets, particularly those with other conditions, may be most at risk.

If your ferret shows symptoms of the green slime virus, take him to a veterinarian immediately. He or she will make sure that the ferret does not become dehydrated and that his vital electrolyte balances are maintained. The vet may also prescribe antibiotics to prevent secondary infections from setting in.

Even after the worst of the disease is over, a ferret may remain thin and have soft, poorly formed stools for several months. Ferrets who have recovered from the green slime virus may remain carriers of the virus for eight months or longer, so they should not have contact with other ferrets who have not had the disease.

Currently, there is no way to prevent this disease other than by separating your ferret from infected ferrets. However, researchers at the Armed Forces Institute of Pathology are attempting to isolate and replicate the virus that causes the green slime disease in hopes that a vaccine eventually can be developed.

and coughing, decreased appetite, and perhaps diarrhea. As with humans, the tried-and-true treatment is rest and plenty of fluids. But skip the advice in the old maxim, "Take two aspirin and call me in the morning." Do not give aspirin to your ferret except under instructions from your veterinarian. Never give aspirin substitutes such as ibuprofen or acetaminophen to your ferret.

Certain conditions may require a closer look by your vet. If your ferret has a fever, a greenish or yellowish discharge from his ears or nose, a loss of appetite, or if the coldlike symptoms last for more than five days, take him to your veterinarian. Your ferret may have developed a secondary bacterial infection that could require antibiotics, or he may need fluids or other medical support.

Ferrets (like skunks, dogs, and even cats) are born with a pair of anal scent glands, one on either side of the anal opening. These glands can become clogged.

A ferret experiencing discomfort associated with his anal scent glands may scratch or rub his anal area on the carpet, a behavior sometimes described as scooting. You may also feel one or two raised bumps near his anus.

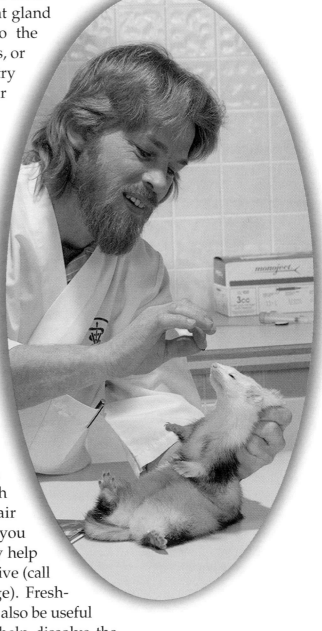

This veterinarian is demonstrating a good way to administer oral medication to a ferret.

You may be able to help unclog a scent gland by applying warm, wet compresses to the area. Your vet may also be able to express, or squeeze, a clogged gland—but don't try this yourself. If the gland is infected, your vet may prescribe antibiotics.

Left untreated, an infected anal scent gland can become so swollen that it actually ruptures. If that occurs, your ferret will need to have the affected gland removed and may require a few stitches to close the wound. If clogged or infected scent glands are a recurring problem, your veterinarian will probably recommend that the ferret have both glands removed.

Hair balls are another common problem for ferrets. As with cats, hair balls are caused by hair swallowed during grooming. Unlike cats, however, ferrets rarely rid themselves of hair balls by vomiting, and surgical removal of a hair ball is sometimes necessary.

Hair balls in the stomach can make a ferret feel full, so he may not eat as much as he should. Chronic irritation from hair balls can even lead to stomach ulcers. If you suspect your ferret has a hair ball, it may help to administer a small amount of cat laxative (call your veterinarian for the proper dosage). Fresh-squeezed papaya or pineapple juice may also be useful because the enzymes they contain can help dissolve the

Like cats, ferrets can get hair balls from grooming. Luckily many ferrets find the remedy, a laxative for cats, very tasty.

matrix that holds the hair together. See your veterinarian if the problem continues.

As a precautionary measure, some veterinarians recommend that you give your ferret a quarter to half a teaspoon of a hair-ball preventive (the kind made for cats) two or three times a week, and every day during the two annual shedding seasons.

The Digestive System

Your ferret may not fight rush-hour traffic to the office every day, but he can develop stomach ulcers. If your ferret has ulcers, he may show signs of abdominal distress such as teeth grinding; lethargy; loss of appetite; weight loss; and black, tarry stools. Vomiting may also occur occasionally.

Just as stomach ulcers in humans have been shown to be related to bacteria in the stomach, another bacterium (*Helicobacter mustelae*) is thought to cause ulcers in ferrets. Your veterinarian is likely to treat the condition with antibiotics and medicines that coat the stomach. The ferret may require extra tender loving care—and perhaps even hand-feeding—until his appetite returns.

In addition to the bright green diarrhea of ECE, ferrets can suffer from ordinary diarrhea, which is a symptom of several ailments such as a viral or bacterial infection, or the coccidia parasite. Lymphosarcoma, a cancer of the lymph glands, can also cause diarrhea. Or your ferret could simply have eaten too much of something, such as milk or a milk product, for which his digestive tract is ill equipped.

Diarrhea may cause ferrets to dehydrate quickly. If the diarrhea lasts more than twenty-four hours or is accompanied by other symptoms, don't take chances—call your vet. Of course, if the diarrhea is bright green, or if you suspect the ferret may have been exposed to the green slime virus, take your ferret to the vet immediately!

Chewing fanatics that they are, ferrets are prone to nibbling and swallowing just about anything they encounter. Unfortunately, nonfood objects may not be able to pass through a ferret's system and instead may get lodged in

Make sure ferret toys are too large to be swallowed and are made of materials that cannot be broken or torn.

his stomach or small intestine. A piece of a rubber toy, a bit of foam, or even a rubber band can become a life-threatening danger.

A ferret with an intestinal blockage may show discomfort or tenderness in his belly and may paw at his mouth, a sign of nausea. Vomiting or an attempt to vomit is another common symptom. A mucous stool indicates the intestine is secreting material to try to soothe a lining that may be irritated by a foreign object, while a black, tarry stool indicates intestinal bleeding. A bloody stool indicates trauma to the large intestine or colon. If your ferret is not eliminating stools at all, the intestine may be completely obstructed.

If you think your ferret has an intestinal obstruction, take him to your veterinarian. Don't wait to see how things are tomorrow; tomorrow may be too late. Immediate surgery may be necessary. Your veterinarian may take X rays to try to pinpoint the source of the trouble, but unfortunately, X rays do not always pick up intestinal obstructions. The vet may have to make a tentative diagnosis based on the ferret's symptoms.

Surgery to remove an intestinal blockage is expensive for you and no fun at all for a ferret. Prevention is the best of all possible cures. Take ferret proofing seriously and resist the temptation to give your ferret those cute but dangerous chewable rubber and soft plastic toys.

Geriatric Conditions

Ferrets are considered old when they reach the age of four. They may develop a variety of diseases as they age, including kidney failure, heart disease, and several forms of cancer. Sometimes they suffer from several illnesses at once. For more detailed information, or for a diagnosis of your pet's particular symptoms, be sure to consult your vet.

When kidney function breaks down, ferrets tend to drink and urinate more frequently than normal. They

If you notice your ferret drinking or urinating more than usual, you should have him checked by a vet for kidney disease.

Ten Important Warning Signs for Ferrets of All Ages

If your ferret exhibits any of the following warning signs, he should be seen by your veterinarian promptly.

Pale Gums

Gums should appear pink and healthy. To test, apply gentle pressure to the gums. They should rapidly return to pink. Pale gums or slow capillary refill time may indicate anemia, shock, septicemia, or a heart condition.

Dehydration

Like the skin on the back of your hand, a ferret's skin should rebound quickly after a gentle pinch. Skin that rebounds slowly indicates the animal is dehydrated. (Aging will cause some loss of elasticity as well.) Dehydration may indicate kidney disease. Ferrets with the green slime virus are extremely susceptible to dehydration.

Low Response to Pain

To test your ferret's response to pain, pinch his toe. Your ferret should pull his leg back. If there is no response or a delayed response, it may indicate spinal or nerve damage.

Lethargy or Appetite Loss

Sluggishness or lack of appetite can be a warning sign of various illnesses, including severe infection, heartworm disease, insulinoma, adrenal tumor, heart disease, or kidney disease. Tiring quickly while playing is a symptom of heart disease. Weight loss can indicate kidney disease or lymphosarcoma.

Vomiting

Gagging or actual vomiting are symptomatic of a variety of problems, ranging from hair balls or swallowing an indigestible object to ulcers, stomach cancer, liver disease, kidney disease, lymphosarcoma, or insulinoma.

Rapid or Difficult Breathing

Rapid breathing is a warning sign of heart disease while difficult breathing is a symptom of heartworm disease and lymphosarcoma.

Back Leg Weakness

A dragging or drooping rear leg may indicate low blood sugar, insulinoma, or neurological trauma. Muscle atrophy indicates adrenal tumors.

Sudden Collapse

If your ferret suddenly collapses, he may suffer from heart disease or lymphosarcoma. Seizure, coma, or staring off into space are signs of insulinoma.

Loss of Hair

Loss of hair along the back, tail, and rump that is not associated with molting indicates adrenal tumors. Hair loss may also result from external parasites or a low-quality diet.

Diarrhea

Diarrhea is a symptom of viral or bacterial infections and lymphosarcoma. If green, it indicates the green slime virus in which case you should contact your vet immediately.

---

can lose coordination and become lethargic. Other signs of kidney disease may include bad breath, mouth sores, depression, and dehydration. In the later stages of the disease, ferrets may experience weakness, dehydration, loss of appetite, weight loss, and vomiting. They also may have tarry stools.

Cystic calculi, deposits of mineral crystals (called stones) that narrow or block the flow of urine through the urethra, also sometimes occur in ferrets. While the problem can affect both male and female ferrets, it tends to be noted more often in males. The condition may result from feeding a ferret an inappropriate diet such as dog food.

Ferrets also can develop bacterial cystitis, an infection

of the bladder caused by one of several types of *E. coli* bacteria. Your veterinarian will culture the urine to isolate the offender and can prescribe antibiotics to treat this problem.

Cardiomyopathy—the thickening, thinning, or stiffening of the walls of the heart, which interferes with the heart's ability to properly pump blood—is also a relatively common problem in ferrets aged four and older. Experts do not know the exact cause of heart disease, although (as with humans) diet may be a contributing factor.

Cancers such as insulinoma, lymphosarcoma, and adrenal tumors are a leading cause of death in ferrets. Experts estimate that cancer will strike more than half—and perhaps close to three-quarters—of all ferrets. Many types of cancer tend to develop in ferrets over the age of four. A ferret may have more than one type of cancer at a time. Fortunately, many cancers can be controlled, if not cured, with surgery or drugs.

An insulinoma is a tumor of the pancreas that causes excess insulin production, which in turn leads to low blood sugar levels—the opposite of diabetes. This cancer is a fairly common disease in ferrets, with an estimated one-third or more of ferrets developing it in later life.

Assembling a Basic Ferret First Aid Kit

Having these basic supplies on hand will help you handle common medical emergencies.

Hydrogen peroxide for cleaning wounds

Betadine antiseptic for wounds

Benadryl Children's Elixir for allergic reactions (call your vet for dosage instructions before administering)

Cat laxative for constipation and hair balls

Cotton balls and swabs for cleaning wounds

Gauze and bandages for bandaging wounds

Styptic powder to stop bleeding

Feeding syringe and soft food (such as Gerber's Second Meals Chicken baby food or Hills Prescription Diet a/d) for hand-feeding

Rectal thermometer and K/Y Jelly or other lubricant for taking your ferret's temperature (note: normal temperature for a ferret is 101 to 102.5 degrees Fahrenheit)

A spray bottle to prevent overheating

A travel cage made up with a soft blanket for transporting your ferret to the vet

Karo Syrup, Nutrical, or honey if your ferret has been diagnosed with an insulinoma (ask your vet to show you how to administer)

Feeding ferrets foods that are high in sugar (cookies, ice cream, and the like) can contribute to the development of this disease.

Lymphosarcoma is a cancer of the lymph glands. Ferrets have lymph glands in a variety of locations in their bodies, including in the armpits, along the neck, behind the knees, and toward the base of the abdomen near the hind legs. This cancer strikes both young and old ferrets, but may progress more swiftly in younger ferrets. In older ferrets, it is a chronic, wasting disease.

Adrenal tumors are either benign or cancerous tumors affecting one or both of the tiny adrenal glands located near a ferret's kidneys. These tumors cause the adrenal glands to secrete excess hormones, tricking the ferret into some rather unusual displays. Spayed females may go through a simulated heat, and neutered males may exhibit male sexual behaviors such as aggression. There may also be mammary (breast) development in both males and females.

Adrenal tumors are a fairly common ferret disorder, with an estimated one-quarter of all ferrets developing this

This ferret is curiously investigating a first aid kit.

disease, typically after the age of three. Diagnosis may be made through a physical exam, ultrasound, or exploratory surgery. Again, some ferret experts suspect genetics could play a part in this disease.

Handling Common Emergencies

Given the ferret's boisterous and curious nature, you're apt to have to deal with some household emergencies. It's likely that at some point your ferret's nail will tear and bleed. This happens when the vein in a ferret's nail is cut or clipped. If the nail has broken, use nail clippers to gently snip away any dangling piece that did not break off completely and clean the area with a cotton ball soaked in hydrogen peroxide. Use styptic powder (or if that's not available, bar soap, cornstarch, or flour) to stop the bleeding. If you can't get the bleeding to stop, or if signs of infection such as swelling and discharge develop later, take your ferret to your veterinarian.

Occasionally, a ferret will rip away the entire nail from his toe, which can result in serious bleeding. Apply direct pressure to the foot to stop or at least slow the bleeding, and take the ferret to a veterinarian as soon as possible. The injury may require cauterization to stop the bleeding.

Be gentle when trimming a ferret's nails, especially if you're trimming away a broken nail.

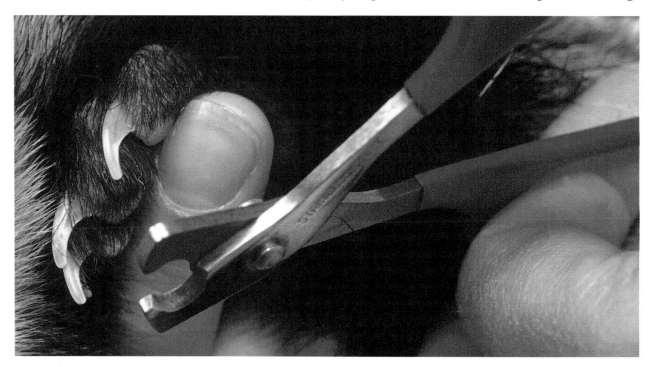

This sable ferret's injured leg is being bandaged; however, only a veterinarian should set a broken bone.

If someone accidentally steps or sits on your ferret, he will let you know by wailing. Try to determine whether the ferret is seriously hurt or just frightened. Pay close attention to his behavior for the next few hours. If he does not quickly resume normal play and eating activities, or if you see any evidence that he is in pain, the ferret should be seen by your veterinarian immediately to determine if he has broken bones and/or internal injuries.

Ferrets who love to chew on lamp cords or other electrical wires may be unpleasantly surprised by such "toys." Electrical shock can cause severe burns, neurological shock, and even death. If your ferret has been shocked by an electrical cord, keep him warm (but not overheated) to minimize nervous shock, and take him to your vet immediately. Carefully unplug the appliance; it may be necessary to shut off the circuit breaker to do so safely. Be sure

A ferret will explore everywhere, so good ferret proofing is a must. Keep toxic chemicals and poisons, even your garbage, out of your ferret's reach.

to repair or replace the cord before using the appliance again to prevent any further shocks or an electrical fire.

Another danger is poisoning from household chemicals under your sink. These chemicals can be irresistibly appealing to ferrets. If your ferret manages to swallow something toxic and you can't get in touch with your veterinarian, you can reach the National Animal Poison Control Center, a twenty-four-hour, nonprofit service staffed by veterinarians, at 900-680-0000 (you will be charged $20.00 for the first five minutes and $2.95 for each additional minute) or 800-548-2423 (have a credit card ready. The charge is a flat $30.00 for each call). You may want to write these numbers in your phone book right under your veterinarian's number.

Breeding

To do it justice, the subject of breeding ferrets would require a book unto itself. Breeding is a highly complex and demanding undertaking that is not recommended for novices. Breeders have a tremendous responsibility both for the well-being of their breeding pairs and for the healthy development of the offspring. It takes time, patience, expertise, and plenty of just plain hard work—consider the amount of cage cleaning alone!

Before you decide that you want to breed ferrets, think seriously about what you expect from the job. Despite the price of pet store ferrets, breeding is not a quick

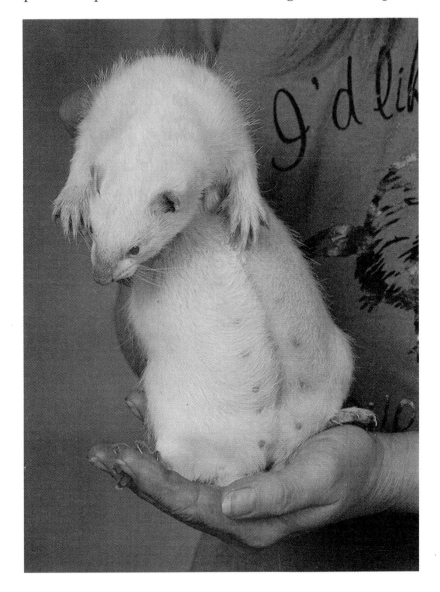

A pregnant jill can give birth to a litter of one to more than fifteen kits.

A one-day-old kit is small enough to fit in a teaspoon. The helpless kit weighs only 8 to 10 grams at birth.

money-making opportunity. You can run up a very high vet bill if a jill requires a C-section or a litter needs to be altered and possibly de-scented. And there's always a risk of losing your breeding females to birth complications. In addition to vet bills, expenses for food, cages, and vaccines can add up in a hurry. You may need to acquire a business license, and if you make more than $500 each year retail, or any amount selling wholesale, you will need a USDA permit as well. And don't overlook the necessary record keeping that goes along with the endeavor.

If the mother has a plentiful milk supply, a kit may triple his weight in ten days. Pictured here is a two-week-old kit.

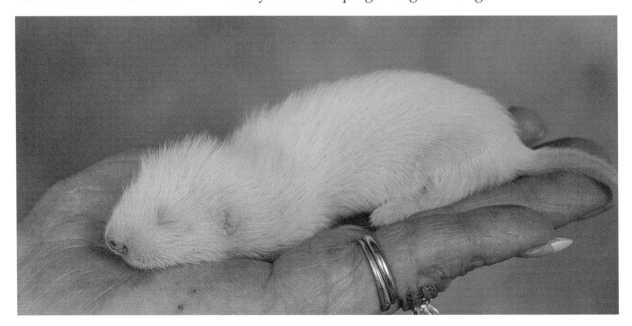

At seven weeks, this kit has been weaned.

Other aspects of ferret breeding should be considered. Do you have sufficient expertise to meet your ferrets' needs? Can you cope with the emotional ups and downs that come with helping jills through the birth process and sometimes watching kits die from causes beyond your control? On a more philosophical note, consider the current pet overpopulation crisis we face with cats and dogs. Too many ferrets already wind up in shelters. Are you confident that the pets you would be bringing into the world would always have good homes?

Don't keep your ferret unaltered thinking you may want to breed ferrets some time down the road. Remember, female ferrets in particular face serious health risks if they're neither spayed nor bred. And hobs may become aggressive to other ferrets (both male and female) during the mating season.

If you are serious about wanting to become a breeder, first find out everything you can about ferrets. Join your local ferret club. Volunteer at a shelter. Read every book on ferrets you can get your hands on. And ask a nearby breeder if you can help out, particularly during the breeding season.

Be sure to find out what permits and licenses are required to become a breeder where you live, and don't forget to inquire about local zoning requirements.

Legal and Regulatory Concerns

As of the end of the twentieth century, ferrets are still illegal to keep as pets in California, Hawaii, and the District of Columbia. It's illegal to sell ferrets in South Carolina, although it's legal to own them there. And, as stated earlier, ferrets are banned or restricted on the local level in some cities and counties across the nation. While so far there has been little movement toward changing the status of owning ferrets in Hawaii, efforts to legalize ferrets have been under way in California for some time. Ferret activists in that state continue to hope that the situation will change in the not-too-distant future.

Laws prohibiting ferrets are generally based on three concerns: a fear that ferrets may escape and breed in the

In some parts of the country ferrets are illegal to own as pets. Check the local laws in your area before bringing a ferret home.

wild, harming native plants and animals; the belief that ferrets may be dangerous, particularly to infant children; and the fear that ferrets may transmit rabies. Based on one or more of these concerns, legislators may target ferrets alone or may erroneously lump domestic ferrets together with prohibited wild and exotic animals.

Check it Out

One way to learn more about the legal status of ferrets where you live is to join your local ferret club. Ferret organizations—along with your veterinarian—are usually good sources of information. But don't stop there.

- Check with your state wildlife agency, often called the Department of Fish & Game or Department of the Environment

- Check with your zoning department to determine whether there are restrictions on keeping certain pets—or a total number of pets—in your area

- Stay on top of local legislation—contact your city council, board of supervisors, and animal-control division

- Talk to your state's Department of Agriculture and Department of Natural Resources

- Contact state and local public health agencies

- Find out if your subdivision's local covenants, codes, and restrictions (CC&Rs) contain restrictive provisions concerning animals

---

Ferret advocates firmly dismiss each of these concerns as meritless and correctly point out that ferrets are *domestic* animals, not tamed wild animals. But a law is the law as long as it is on the books. You should be aware that in areas where ferrets are not legal, they can be confiscated by animal authorities and may be killed—without a court hearing.

Even where ferrets are not banned outright, special rules may apply. You may be required to license, register, spay or neuter, or vaccinate your pet. A small but growing number of local governments are imposing a requirement that certain pets be identified with microchips so the owner can be located if the animal escapes. Under some ordinances, a special license is required to keep exotic pets, including domestic ferrets. Prerequisites to obtaining the license may include a home inspection by animal-control authorities and a special hearing before a licensing board. Your local government may have other restrictions or requirements as well.

Keep in mind that the regulatory environment is constantly changing. It is important that you stay current on actual and potential changes in the law at both state and local levels. Locate groups in your area that follow legislative and regulatory issues affecting ferret owners.

It's always a good idea to obtain a copy of the law, ordinance, or other document regarding ferret ownership. It's up to you to stay abreast of changes in the laws affecting pets and to let your elected officials know how you feel about the laws.

Ferrets sometimes seem to have a better grasp on life than we humans. If ferrets ruled the world, there would be a lot more time devoted to playing and exploring and a lot less spent on jobs, homework, and chores. Not a bad idea, really.

That special ferret attitude can't help but bring a touch of playfulness and joy to the most humdrum of households. As much as ferrets add to our lives, we owe them the best of our love and care in turn.

This book is intended as a solid introduction to ferrets and ferret issues—a sort of Ferrets 101. But don't stop your education here. Other good resources include ferret clubs, shelter organizations, magazines, and even the Internet. New information about ferrets—their care, health, and legal status—is being generated all the time.

Now, go play with a ferret. Work can wait.

Ferrets love to play and crawl through tubes. Give them safe toys that will fuel their curiosity.

Photo Fun

Do you want a formal portrait of your ferret to mail to your in-laws, tape on your school locker, or frame for your desk at work? Or would you just like to capture a ferret moment to share with friends? Here are some tips from professional animal photographer Reneé Stockdale.

- Be ready! That perfect shot could materialize at any time. Keep a camera handy in the room where you normally play with your ferret. And remember, a ferret's attention span is brief.

- Know your ferret's routine. If your ferret usually wakes up around a certain hour, that may be the time to catch a sleepy yawn. If she's hungry or intent on exploring a new room, it's probably useless to try to interest her in staying still for the camera.

- Familiar toys and familiar places will help put your ferret at ease. On the other hand, any new toy or object is cause for investigation.

- While ferrets are not constitutionally geared for sitting still while you focus the camera, a dab of Linatone on a toy or table surface may get your ferret's attention long enough for a shot. You may also find that a firm, repeated "stay" command can help, especially if you practice during nonphotograph hours. Be prepared to practice until your ferret gets the idea, reinforcing the "stay" command by gently returning her to the desired position each time she strays.

- Use an assistant. Those cute portraits of a ferret sitting up often require someone away from the camera. An assistant can also help reinforce the "stay" command.

Reward good behavior with lavish praise—a few seconds of staying put is a terrific accomplishment for a ferret.

Try to compose your picture so that the ferret completely fills the frame. If you are using a fixed-focus camera, however, know your minimum focusing distance and be careful not to get too close, or other important subjects in the picture (a toy, for example) may be blurry.

To avoid red-eye, try to catch your ferret looking away from the camera rather than directly at it, or use an off-camera flash.

Don't be afraid to practice. Buy several rolls of high-quality film. Have fun!

CLUBS & ORGANIZATIONS

Ferret enthusiasts all across the country have formed clubs and organizations devoted to ferrets. Many of these organizations issue newsletters, provide ferret health and care information, sponsor ferret shows, and sell supplies. They are a great networking resource as well as an invaluable source of practical information.

American Ferret Association (AFA)
P.O. Box 3986
Frederick, MD 21705-3986
(888) 337-7381
www.ferret.org/
e-mail: afa@ferrets.org

Ferret Fanciers Club
711 Chautauqua Ct.
Pittsburgh, PA 15214
(412) 322-1161

FURO (Ferret Unity & Registration Organization, Inc.)
P.O. Box 844
Elon College, NC 27244
(910) 342-7748

Legion of Superferrets National (LOS)
P.O. Box 866
Levittown, PA 19058-0866
(215) 946-2747
Fax: (215) 946-1291
www.ferret-world.csc.peach net.edu.

LIFE (League of Independent Ferret Enthusiasts)
P.O. Box 11007
Burke, VA 20172
(703) 777-2112
www.acmeferret.com/life/

North American Ferret Association
P.O. Box 1963
Dale City, VA 22193-1963
(703) 590-2132
Fax: (703) 730-5131

UFO (United Ferret Organization)
P.O. Box 606
6 Water Street
Assonet, MA 02702
(508) 644-5562
Fax: (508) 644-5201

State and local ferret organizations are too numerous to list here, but there is likely to be one near you. Ask at your local pet store or call one of the national organizations above for a referral.

You'll also want to get acquainted with the Pet Industry Joint Advisory Council (PIJAC). PIJAC serves as the voice of the pet industry—including retail pet stores, pet product manufacturers, and distributors—in government. When legal questions or proposed legislative changes arise, these dedicated people fight to make sure that laws are both fair and reasonable to pet owners and pet professionals. If there is an existing or proposed law affecting ferrets in your area that you believe is unreasonable, you can let the folks at PIJAC know by writing or calling:

Pet Industry Joint Advisory Council (PIJAC)
1220 19th Street, NW, Suite 400
Washington, DC 20036
(202) 452-1525
Fax: (202) 293-4377

While the people at PIJAC can't fight city hall for you, they may be able to connect you with people or organizations in your area working on the same issue. Your call will also help them keep abreast of ferret-related trends and legislative changes across the nation.

SHELTERS & RESCUE ORGANIZATIONS

Ferret shelters and rescue groups not only find homes for lost and abandoned ferrets, they also can be a wonderful source of information about ferret care, ferret products, and veterinarians experienced in ferret medicine. For information on shelters or rescue groups near you, contact:

AFA
(information listed under organizations)

F.A.I.R. (Ferret Adoption, Information & Rescue Society)
1937 S. Mannheim Road
Westchester, IL 60153
(708) 681-3181

Ferrets Etc. (Holistic Ferret Rescue)
4339 South Galapago St.
Englewood, CO 80110
(303) 761-1983
e-mail: ferretsetc@aol.com

STAR* Ferrets (Shelters That Adopt & Rescue Ferrets)
P.O. Box 1714
Springfield, VA 22151-0714
(703) 354-5073
www.optics.rochester.edu:8080/users/pgreene/for-others/database.html
e-mail: STARFeret@aol.com

FERRET MAGAZINES

Thanks to the steadily growing ranks of ferret enthusiasts, a number of consumer magazines and organizations devoted to ferrets have appeared recently. Subscribing to some of these magazines will help you keep in touch with the very latest in ferret information.

Critters USA, Ferrets USA, and Ferrets magazine

The first two are annuals devoted to small animals and ferrets, respectively. *Ferrets* magazine is a bimonthly magazine. All three are available in pet stores. To find out where you can purchase a sample copy of any of these publications, write or call:
P.O. Box 6050
Mission Viejo, CA 92690
(714) 855-8822
Fax: (714) 855-3045

Modern Ferret

A bimonthly magazine for ferret enthusiasts. Available by subscription, or in Borders Books & Music, Barnes & Noble, Tower Records, and pet stores.
P.O. Box 338
Massapequa Park, NY 11762
(516) 799-1364
Fax: (516) 797-4021
www.modernferret.com

FERRETS ON THE INTERNET*

The Internet is a new and fun way to keep up with ferret events and information, and to network with other ferret lovers. Internet addresses are, however, subject to change, and more sites are being added all the time. Here are a few places for you to get started:

Animal Network
www.animalnetwork.com

California Domestic Ferret Association
www.cdfa.com

Ferret Central
www.optics.rochester.edu:8080/users/pgreene/central.html

Ferret FAQ
www.optics.rochester.edu:8080/users/pgreene/faq/index.html

Ferret Mailing List
For information, send e-mail to:
ferret-request@cunyvm.cuny.edu

Ferret Net Home Page
www.Ferret.net/

Net Vet
http://netvet.wush.edu/ferrets.htm

Usenet News Group
alt.pets.ferrets

America Online Ferret Chat
Every Saturday night beginning at 10:00 p.m. EST, there is a two-hour ferret chat in the Pet Care Forum's Animal Talk Room.

Ferret information may also be found in the Message Center under Small Mammals & Exotic Pets in AOL's Pet Care Forum.

Information provided courtesy of Scott Beisner, who operates the Web site for the California Domestic Ferret Association, and by Randy Sellers, chair of the American Ferret Association's Legislative & Legal Affairs Committee.

Glossary

adrenal tumors: either benign or cancerous tumors affecting one or both of the tiny adrenal glands located near the kidneys

alter: to neuter or spay an animal

aplastic anemia: a serious and potentially fatal illness often developed by unspayed, unbred female ferrets. It is characterized by the inability of bone marrow to produce sufficient blood cells.

baseline data: a set of critical medical test data that is later used for comparison or control

booster shot: a supplementary dose of an immunizing agent

canine distemper: a highly contagious viral disease that is received through direct contact with an infected dog

cardiomyopathy: a heart disease characterized by a thickening or stiffening of the walls of the heart, interfering with the heart's ability to pump blood

chemistry panel: screening devices that detect a variety of problems including lymphoma

complete blood count (CBC): a common blood test that screens for a variety of factors

dander: minute scales from an animal's hair or skin that can act as allergens

de-scenting: an operation to remove a ferret's anal scent glands

domesticated: tamed animals who have been selectively bred over hundreds of years for certain characteristics

electrolytes: minerals in the body, such as sodium and potassium, that are necessary for proper cell and nerve function

epizootic catarrhal enteritis (ECE): commonly called the green slime virus or the green diarrhea; a rapidly dehydrating viral infection that affect ferrets

gib: a male ferret who has been neutered

heartworm: a parasite transmitted by mosquitos that grows inside the heart chamber and, if left untreated, can lead to heart damage and death

hob: an unneutered male ferret

intact: not spayed or neutered

insulinoma: a cancer of the pancreas

intestinal impaction: a blockage of the intestine, usually caused by the swallowing of an indigestible object

jill: an unspayed (intact) female ferret

kit: a baby ferret

lymphosarcoma: cancer of the lymph system

metabolism: chemical changes that take place in the body; usually used in terms of changing food to energy

microchip: a radio-wave-activated transponder encased in a tiny glass tube, about the size and shape of a grain of rice, that is inserted under an animal's skin by a veterinarian. A scanner can be used to identify a lost animal equipped with a microchip.

Mustela nigripes: scientific name for the endangered black-footed ferret

Mustela putorius furo: scientific name for the domestic (pet) ferret

prolapsed rectum: a rectum that has been pushed out through the anus and is visible

scruffing: holding a ferret by the loose skin at the scruff of the neck, much the way a mother cat carries a kitten

septicemia: a bacterial infection of the blood that infects a ferret's whole system

sprite: a spayed female ferret

styptic powder: a medicated substance that tends to stop the bleeding of a shallow surface injury

ultrasound: sound waves above the range of human hearing used in a technique to examine a body internally by forming an image on a screen to assist with medical diagnosis, therapy, and surgery

weasel war dance: behavior displayed by a ferret expressing happiness or excitement

Index